To: Johnny + [...]
Keep doing what you love,
with love + passion —

Getting There

1/30/09

Getting There

Driving High Performance Strategies and Tactics for Career Decisions

(It's not about the résumé)

Luis A. Martínez

Gettingtherecoach.com

Library of Congress Control Number: 2008904081
ISBN: Hardcover   978-1-4363-4059-5
               Softcover   978-1-4363-4058-8

Getting There—Driving High Performance Strategies and Tactics for Career Decisions

Luis A. Martínez and The National Resource Group

United States Copyright Office, June 27, 2006
All rights reserved under Title 17, United States Code

The author gratefully acknowledges the quotation from Carlos Eire's book, Waiting for Snow in Havana, excerpted with permission from the Free Press, a division of Simon & Schuster, copyright © 2003, by Simon & Schuster

An excerpt from a newsletter by Michael D. Zinn and Associates is reprinted with permission from Michael D. Zinn & Associates, Princeton, NY, copyright © 2006.

This book is a work of nonfiction. All the stories are true exactly as redacted with permission of those persons depicted. However, some names have been changed for privacy.

Logo design by Amanda MacDonald of Red Horse Design

This book was printed in the United States of America.

To order additional copies of this book, contact:
Xlibris Corporation
1-888-795-4274
www.Xlibris.com
Orders@Xlibris.com
47538

CONTENTS

Question That You Will Be Asked; Those Pesky Behavioral Interviewing Questions; Handling Other Questions That May Arise; Some Questions You Hope They Don't Ask; Illegal Questions That Employers Should Never Ask; Some Exceptions; Two: The T-Chart—Knowing Their Needs and Educating Your Interviewer about Your Contributions; Three: The Questions That You Must Ask; Tips and Tactics for Interviewing; Do's and Don'ts for Interviewing; Handling Rejection; How to Handle Exploratory Interviews; The Purpose of This Interview is—to Get the Next Interview!; What Are They Really Buying? Your Attributes!; It's Really About Turning Your Passion into Opportunity; A Good Interviewer Is Hard to Find; How to Handle the Telephone Interview; Immediately After the Interview; On Exchanging Business Cards; For Exploratory Interviews; For Networking Meetings; What About Working with Headhunters? The New World of E-mail; Homework.

All the incidents and dialogue come straight from God's imagination.
As does the author himself.
And the reader.
Still, all of us are responsible for our own actions.

—An inspiration from Carlos Eire, author of
Waiting for Snow in Havana: Confessions of a Cuban Boy

This book is dedicated to and in memory of my sister

Diana Patricia Martínez

La Habana, Cuba

1951-1957

ACKNOWLEDGMENTS

I have many, many people to thank for this book. As of this edition, I have worked with over two hundred clients. *Client* is the word that I use to describe the business relationship that I maintain with my readers as we work using this book. But *client* is not the right word to describe what all of you mean to me. The truth is that I have learned more from you, my client friends, than you have learned from using this career search process. You shared deep and personal aspects of your life with me. You trusted in me.

And for that—I am ever so grateful.

The list of wonderful people who have helped me includes the following: Jim Arnold, for photo editing; Sharon Bahringer for editing, trademark, and copyright documentation; John Bailey for listening to my rants; Patty Brown, Dena Germano, and Jean Ticen for sharing *The Secret*; Donald Burns for thorough editing and good content ideas; Christine Cody for her publishing tips and insight; Robert Colangelo for his business counsel; Jane Fairchild, for editing and contributions to networking and cold/warm calling; Rachel Gordon for marketing and business development advice; Jim Graham for career advice; Kelly Hayden for her encouraging support; Mike Hazard and Ellyn Tarasuk for designing my website; Richard Holtzberg for his legal counsel; Elaine Johnson for great editing; Christine Kennedy for book jacket design; Timothy Madigan for editing and publishing advice; Cheri Magin for her contribution to the section "The First 100 Days"; Dawn Marchionda for her editing; Augustín Melendez for his encouragement, editing, and advice; Hannah Morgan for her subject matter expertise and advice; Janet Nelson for her project development suggestions; Robert Rosenfeld for his advice on book publishing; Jennifer Sertl for persuading me to clarity; Rosa Smith-Montanaro for their invaluable book publishing expertise and guidance; Samantha Tassone for spontaneously offering to be an Advisor to the Diana Patricia Martinez Memorial Foundation (a 501c(3) related project); Debbie

Vater for her assistance launching the foundation; Mike Waters for his sage advice; Tracy Wowk for her great insights; many clients and friends for their wonderful quotes, advice, and aphorisms; and many more to add as this project grows and evolves.

My parents, Zoila and Jose Luis, have been an inspiration my entire life. Their optimism, their faith in God, their abiding love and unfailing support in all aspects of my life have been invaluable.

And of course, I received constant support from my wife Sharon and my children, Alison, Alexander, and Bradley. They accommodated my crazy schedule when I met with clients and patiently waited for the computer as I spent countless hours writing this book.

Luis Martínez
Pittsford, New York

INTRODUCTION

Change is my opportunity.
—LAM

A job search is a very difficult process for most people. There is so much incertitude, no clear avenues, and no definitive direction. Everything that's important to us seems to be in the hands of strangers. If unemployed, we are very uncomfortable without a job. We don't like the process of presenting ourselves to strangers and trying to persuade them to hire us. This process is very unpleasant, even for the best prepared.

There are factors that impede many people—whether frustrated in their current positions or unemployed—from being productive in their job search. One of them is that they don't know how to go about it. Another one is fear.

This process outlined in this book is designed to help you in your job search by (a) outlining some basic concepts to quickly launch your job search and then (b) providing a tool kit (strategies and tactics) with easy-to-follow directions to improve your confidence and reduce your fear of being unprepared.

In my experience with many clients who have used the process presented in this book, they all have marveled at how easy the concepts are to learn, and how quickly they can turn one or two hours of good work with these tools into a solid, productive job search process with excellent results.

Over the years, I have purchased and read a number of the most popular career-counseling and job search books. Perusing them, I have asked myself, "If I were unemployed, and my wife and children and other dependents were waiting to see my plan for finding work, which of these multihundred-page books would I buy, and where would I begin?" Well, the fact that you have this book in hand makes it easy to answer that question. Begin right here on this page and follow along in the order presented. Read and do everything required in Career Coaching 101 (CC-101). When you're satisfied that

13

you've completed the homework assignment for CC-101, then read and do the required homework for the rest of the chapters.

Even if you don't finish the book, you'll be prepared to approach targeted companies and successfully interview with them as long as you at least read and finish the homework in CC-101 through CC-103.

All of my clients who have done the work required in CC-101, 102, and 103 have found the following:

- They have more confidence in the tools—"elevator speech", resume, and cover letter—needed in order to introduce themselves to potential employers.
- They are more discerning and better able to choose among potential employers.
- They are oftentimes much better prepared for the interview than the hiring managers interviewing them.
- They march in with confidence toward the negotiating table for salary, benefits, and associated perquisites.
- They get all this done and move on to their new career with a better sense of effectiveness and efficiency.
- But most of all, they know they're starting to do work that they love to do.

In your job search, you can choose to sit and ponder and study and delve ever more deeply into different occupations, types of employers or geographies, or an infinite number of details about jobs or job characteristics. Some well-known books go to great lengths to help you understand your skills and experience. Others dwell to a great degree on personality types. However, if you find yourself dwelling on more detail and looking for more data, you will quickly realize that you've run into a condition known as "the law of diminishing returns," meaning that no matter how much more detail and data you gather and much more you explore and drill down at these factors, the results are not significantly greater.

So where do we start? I suggest you start by understanding who you are, and then move toward putting together a tool kit to approach the job search.

This, in short, is the thesis of this book—you need to start with a thorough understanding of who you are.

If you are introspective and know something about yourself, then you can prepare an effective job search campaign. Conversely, if you don't know sufficiently about yourself, your resume and other job search tools may lead you in the wrong direction, and your efforts may result in another miserable job.

An analogy that we can use is sports car racing. Preparing for a race requires planning, a strategy, and many tactics. An expert driver with an unsorted, untried car will have difficulty finishing the race. Likewise, the best-prepared car, completely shaken down and sorted out for a particular race circuit, will have a low probability of finishing, let alone winning, with a rookie or unprepared driver.

As the driver, you have to understand the capabilities and limits of your talent. You must also have a thorough understanding of the capabilities of your race car. Understanding both is necessary for optimal results.

The concept of strategizing, planning, and carrying out or executing tactics is nevertheless true in career decision making. In this instance, you are the driver; but no matter how skilled or experienced you are, you must first plan and prepare for your race. You will need a strategy for the main event. You will need some trusted advisors and helpers (pit crew members), some thorough preparation of your materials and tactics, and some practice laps.

What I hope you get out of this book is help with the entire job search process, end to end, quickly and effectively without encountering the dreaded and time wasting condition of diminishing returns.

Here's how one of my clients reacted to our meeting and my career coaching process about three years ago:

You were the best thing that happened to me all last week.

Tara, what are you talking about? What do you mean by that?

All I have at home are my kids screaming, I can't find a job, I'm behind on my bills, I have creditors knocking at my door threatening repossession. My husband's not doing anything, he's not any help. It's just chaos at home.

Oh, Tara, I'm so sorry things are so bad. But all we did was discuss what you love to do, your attributes, and how you can start your job search. It's just tools.

No—it was hope.

Tara Whitman* during our second meeting.

---

*   Names denoted with an asterisk are fictitious to protect the privacy of my clients, but their stories are true exactly as depicted, with their permission.

ONE

CAREER COACHING 101—Who Are You?

Fundamentals

Begin where you are. Begin now.
—Dr. Norman Vincent Peale, minister/author

Typically, when someone starts looking for work, they think of a company that they'd like to work for. "Oh, I hear that DuPont is a great place to work." Or, "I have a friend who works in HSBC Bank, and she really likes it there." Or, "As a schoolteacher, my first preference would be to work in suburban school district."

That's understandable—imagining ourselves in a workplace that appears to meet our needs. In fact, there are many books available that market that very notion—"the best 100 companies to work for" or "the top 100 fastest-growing careers." Many who approach their job search in this manner in fact succeed, that is, they get a top one hundred job in their workplace of first choice, only to find out months later that they've made a big mistake. How does that happen?

It happens because they went about it from the outside in—instead of from the inside out.

Think about what happens when you drop a pebble in a pond. The nucleus of the activity is where the pebble strikes the water. From that point, concentric circles form and travel outward in all directions. Similarly, the first step in your career search is to understand yourself, as the nucleus of the activity. Who are you—in a professional sense?

Some of the questions that you must ask yourself are these: What interests you? What compels you to action? What sorts of activities do you enjoy? What do you love to do?

Identify your passion in life—what kind of work would you do,
for little or no pay, because you just love doing it?

Interests

Focus on your interests, not jobs or positions. Think introspectively about the sort of person that you are. Knowing who you are will help define the kinds of places that you would want, or not want, to work in. Remember the pebble in the water—that's you at your core, with your favorite activities, your talents displayed, and your *attributes* demonstrated (more on this later).

- Think of

    o   what you **love to do**,
    o   the **skills** necessary to do it, and
    o   your **attributes**.

Discovering What You Love to Do

You've got to find what you love.
—Steve Jobs, founder Apple, Inc., NeXT and Pixar

Surely you have sat and wondered what it would be like doing a job that you love to do—and getting paid for it. You may have sat with a cup of coffee during a nice afternoon in your family room and thought, *Why can't I find a job where I can be really happy?* After careful consideration, you may have deemed that to be an unachievable dream, and then, with a deep sigh, you settle for your current reality.

Well, it's time to turn that dream into reality.

With this book I want to help you by asking you to read and record, read and write using the homework sections at the end of the first few chapters, so you can see tangible results quickly. Follow this process, and by the time you finish the first chapter, you'll have some tools in hand. By the end of the second chapter, you'll be ready to write to companies and request interviews.

By the end of the third chapter, if you have done the homework, you'll come across very impressively to your interviewers.

Let's get to work.

ATTENTION: THIS IS THE MOST IMPORTANT THING IN THIS BOOK THAT YOU WILL DO TO HELP YOURSELF!

- Sit down with a pen and a paper and think about a time in a particular job when you loved what you were doing:

  o *What* were you doing, specifically?
  o *Where* were you?
  o Who were the *people involved*?
  o *Why is it precisely that you loved this activity*? Some examples: You love selling jewelry at Lord & Taylor because you really enjoy the smiles of the customers when they purchase a piece; or you love personal training because you see the progress that your clients are making with weight loss, healthier eating habits, and physical fitness; or you love closing a multimillion-dollar deal because of the challenges of the complexity, the intellect of the parties involved and the sweet rewards of a large commission.
  o *What are your strengths?* Many career-counseling guides place emphasis on strengths. It's a safe bet that if you have strengths, in say, organization, coordination, and interpersonal skills, it's easy for you love to work as an events planner.
  o *What behaviors do you see in yourself* that make you believe you are good at what you do?
  o *Which results or positive outcomes* in your work experience demonstrate that you're good at what you're doing?

- Make sure you think about and enumerate those things that you *don't* enjoy.

  o *Understanding what you're not good at*, or does not make you happy, is just as important as what you love to do. If you love to work on teams, you'll be unhappy in a back office in a cubicle by yourself. However, if you can't concentrate with people walking in and interrupting your thought process, then you'll be more productive in a back office in a cubicle by yourself.

o   Chances are that if you are intelligent and well educated, you can land many types of positions, including positions that are wrong for you, positions that you regret later unless you have clearly defined them as careers you will not pursue.

- This process of defining exactly what you love to do *is a lot like writing a letter to a trusted friend.*
- Many clients, when asked to do this type of introspection, will respond, "Gee, I have never thought about it. This is hard. Where do I start?"
- Start by pretending you are telling your best friend about those things you love to do. Pretend you're writing a letter to your old high school or college friend and you want to tell them how you're doing, in terms of work—what you love to do, where you've been most successful and most satisfied.
- *Do not constrain yourself!* This is not the time to think, *Well, I've always loved to cook, and everyone loves my gourmet dishes, but I shouldn't begin by saying I love to cook. That's not really important.* Well, actually that is *most* important because what follows is the question, "*Why* do you love to cook?" Then, many a client will enthusiastically answer this question by saying, "Oh, I love *researching* new recipes, *making* a shopping list, *inviting* some friends over for a dinner, *organizing* all the ingredients, *coordinating* all the different dishes, *managing* the kitchen while my guests are socializing, thinking of *creative* ways to present the meal, *exploring* different wine pairings and finally, *accepting* all the compliments when it all *results* in a great dining experience for them." It's obvious from this brief interchange that cooking is very important to this person, and that it takes a significant amount of work and coordination to create a dining experience. So the importance lies in the fact that this is the foundation for the type of work this person would like—work that involves initiative, research, exploration, creativity, problem solving, coordination, timing, socializing, and event management. And you thought she was just—cooking.
- By definition, *hobbies are activities that we enjoy for their own sake.* Rarely do they yield any income (my hobby, sports car racing *requires* a cash inflow!). But all hobbies—volunteer work, coaching children's sports, community work—all such activities are significant indicators

of (a) what we love to do, *pro bono*, and (b) what we're instinctively good at doing.

- While you're writing down what you love to do, it's not enough to say, "I like working with people." Or, "I like numbers." Or, "I like project management." You need to clarify your ideal work situation; you need to visualize your dream job (more on visualization later).

- In your attempt to catalog what you like, you need to be very specific. (You should also know what you don't like). If you like working with numbers, is it because you like solving mathematical problems, as in engineering or entering debits and credits on ledgers? Is it doing regression analysis of compensation data, or is it decoding enemy-coded messages? If you like working with people, do you mean as a physician, as a retail sales clerk, or as a member of the clergy? And even within those categories, there are other subcategories which can be derived. You can be very specialized; for example, you may love working as lay clergy with incarcerated pregnant women.

Environments

Shop for culture.
—Denise Johnson, Human Resources professional

As you make your list of what you love to do, you should think about the types of environments (not companies) where you would love to work. Every work environment has a culture. What type of culture would you love to work in? Even in a midsized city, there are hundreds of potential work settings that you could approach. How do you differentiate? Where do you start?

Start with environments. What sorts of physical spaces appeal to you? By that I mean, can you picture yourself working in a law firm? Would you be interested in the home construction industry? What about a position in retail department stores (as different from supermarkets)? Would a large manufacturing complex be appealing to you?

Those are different environments. It's just as important to know what you want (say, architectural firms), as what you don't want (emergency room administration).

Envision the types of *environments* where you would be comfortable working. Even the same genre can take many forms, for example:

- *Construction sites, outdoors*—wearing hard hat and boots, clearing land for excavating sites, supervising, surveying for commercial property, civil engineering projects, and offshore rig construction.
- *Construction sites, indoors*—project management, residential construction, building inspection, safety investigation for subsidized community projects.
- *Retail*—local restaurant, high-end boutique, hardware depot, farmer's market.
- *Academic*—private, expensive, preparatory school, downtown public school, marine research laboratory, teaching hospital.
- *Legal*—three-person practice, fifty-person practice, Legal Aid Society, corporate in-house counsel.
- *Healthcare*—rural public health, hospice care, coronary intensive care, nursing school faculty.

The point is that the more specific you are about the activities that you love to do, the better you will understand what kinds of positions you will, or will not, pursue.

Advanced Technique

One way to understand the culture of the company that you are considering is to ask the hiring manager or the human resources manager to describe their company in terms of the Myers-Briggs Type Indicator (MBTI). The MBTI is a personality questionnaire designed to identify certain psychological differences using typological and personality theories of Carl Jung.

If you've ever taken the MBTI, then you know your own personality type. With that information in hand, you may want to ascertain if your targeted company wants or needs the type of person you are. You would ask yourself, Am I going to assimilate well into this environment, given the overall company culture as expressed in terms of the MBTI?

The foregoing is an "advanced" technique, and it only works if both you, as the candidate and the person on the other side of the desk representing the company are well acquainted with this personality assessment tool. However, this method and tool are certainly not essential in discerning among corporate environments.

Okay, so you're ready to try visualization to enable improvements in your work life. But what's that you say, you don't know what it is you want?

Well, here is how you begin to explore this most important aspect of your job search and find an answer for yourself.

The next step is of crucial importance to help yourself. Turn toward the back of this book and use attachment A to write down specific activities that you love to do, for example:

- o Presenting to customers
- o Closing a deal
- o Developing corporate strategy
- o Teaching piano
- o Purchasing goods or services
- o Organizing large complex conventions
- o Keeping books and finance ledgers
- o Investing pension assets
- o Creating marketing collaterals
- o Writing software
- o Recruiting nurses
- o Conducting safety inspections
- o Fundraising

And make sure you write in *complete sentences*, including the specific reasons *why* you love doing this activity.

This is crucial.

The whole point is to understand *why* you love to do certain things. If you just write "sales" or "teaching" or "carpentry," you will not have captured the fundamental, intrinsic incentives that are inherent for you in that activity.

Write complete sentences like this: "I love speech therapy because I can see the progress the patient makes from deficits in oral communication to a fully functioning person, and then, they can move on with their life in a healthy, complete way."

Maybe you like to work alone. "I love to work from home, writing software, because my children are off to school, I have everything I need nearby, I can take care of the phone and e-mail on my own timing, and no one is coming around my "office" to bother me with chitchat and wasting my time."

Or, "I love selling expensive yachts because I love to be near those magnificent machines on the water, I love the intelligence of the buyers, the fact that they've been very successful at their businesses, and with them I have to assemble very complex deals and bring them to closure. Then I love to get a ride in their new yacht."

Deal Busters

You must understand those things that are deal breakers for you. Maybe one consideration as you look for work is that you need flexibility to run errands for an ailing parent. Or maybe you do your best work at 2:00 a.m., so you need the ability to take a laptop home to prepare your work and deliver your best results. Or if you are bored just maintaining current-state processes, then mature companies will likely be boring for you. In that case, it's important for you to understand—is that company you have in mind still growing and evolving? Does it have the technology, business problem, or technical challenges that excite you?

Make sure you understand whether you can travel, how long a commute you can handle, whether you can work weekends or the second shift, etc.

In other words, the more specific you are about your needs and constraints, the more likely you are to zero in on the type of environment where you'll be most successful.

For Recent High School or College Graduates

If you have just graduated from high school or college and you have little or no experience with the work world, the same thinking process still has value.

What activities have you enjoyed while in school?

- Did you like organizing an overnight class trip?
- Did you enjoy being class treasurer?
- Were competitive sports your passion?
- Did you enjoy coursework in art history?
- List those activities that you enjoyed in class, especially extracurricular activities, such as: writing for the school newspaper, coordinating the junior prom, or participating in competitive sports.
- List those job duties that you loved to do in your part-time work or summer internship: taking care of customers at a fast food concession, monitoring activities for summer camp students, working with

engineers on a design proposal, organizing a computerized spreadsheet of all current vendors.

Take an inventory of those things you were excited to do, make sure you spell them out in your resume and cover letter (see Homework for CC-101 at the end of this chapter.) Let the reader or trusted advisor see what you are good at and the reasons you think you are good at it, e.g., your accomplishments. You will learn how to do that in the homework section.

Recognizing and Recording Your Skills

Let's return to attachment A. In your schooling and in your work experience, you have acquired job-related skills. Some are very tangible, e.g., repairing truck diesel engines; others are less tangible—customer relationship management. Sit down and make a list: what skills have you learned that you are qualified to do?

> *Skills are those things you have learned which you can teach to others or you can turn into cash!*
> —LAM

Write down as many skills as you can think of in attachment A. These are some examples:

o   Personal Computing, e.g., Microsoft Office Suite, Access database management, etc.
o   Corporate tax auditing
o   Guidance Counselor, elementary schools
o   Web Development, furniture brokerage
o   Six Sigma Black Belt, health care
o   Electrician, commercial
o   Certified Project Manager, insurance
o   Sous Chef, Thai foods
o   Brand management, sports drink industry
o   Certified Home Health Aide, pediatrics
o   Customer Service Representative, airlines
o   Administrative Assistant, banking
o   Investor Relations, corporate.

Job-related skills, such as the ones listed above, are often learned via traditional schooling and professional and academic credentialing. They are a critical component of your professional life, but don't stop there.

When recording your skills, don't forget to list skills that you have developed which you are using outside of work. For example:

o   Martial Arts Instructor
o   Basketball Coach
o   Emergency Medical Technician
o   Ski Patrol
o   Volunteer Fire Fighter
o   Sign language interpreter
o   Church treasurer
o   Literacy volunteer
o   Magician
o   Dance instructor
o   Poet
o   Teacher of English as a Foreign Language (TOEFL)
o   Sports car racer

Why are these hobbies relevant, you ask? Because they are born of your love for certain activities, aspects of which sometimes (not always) can be a source of gratification and satisfaction in the job as well. They invariably point to your interests, your proclivities, your areas of heartfelt dedication.

In fact, the more "your heart is in it," the more you are likely to be successful at this chosen activity.

Pardon my passion.
—LAM

By the way, I make no apologies for bringing the words *love* and *passion* and *heart* into this discussion. Mine is not some softheaded, bleeding-heart approach to life. On the contrary, read About the Author on the back flap of the jacket of this book, and you'll see that my life has been anything but soft.

Select any individual with world-class accomplishments in any line of work or vocation, be it a professional golfer or a money-making master in Wall Street, a world renowned chef, or celebrated open heart surgeon. If you sit down with them and have a frank conversation, they will soon describe their chosen work using words like *love*, *passion*, and *heartfelt*.

Recognize *Interests*—Don't Settle for Positions

Interests (born of)	Positions (governed by)
Love to do—those things that we would do for free, if we were independently wealthy.	**Title / company / status**—those glittering objects of pride or desire, which soothe our ego and impress the neighbors, but are not tied directly to our core values.
Values—the way we view the world, our "religion."	**Short-term exigencies, pressures**—bills to pay, career ladders to climb, need to impress the in-laws.
Aspirations—what we dreamed about as we were growing up and even into adulthood.	**Subrogated to terms and conditions**—put on the back burner, left to do when we retire, set aside while we hold a job just to make money.
Ambitions—healthy desires for professional growth and development.	**Succumbing to concerns, fears, constraints, avoidance**—accepting jobs out of fear of failure in a career, constraining ourselves thinking we are not desirable or believable, avoiding choices that require some front-end work for a more rewarding future.
Talents—what we were good at before we went to school.	**Schooled skills**—always necessary but not always sufficient, subject to technological changes and economic turns.
Attributes—who we are, the reason we are loved—or not loved.	**Work experience**—learned skills as practiced over time, experiences in certain situations that are likely to reoccur in workplaces, wisdom as related to operational. Activities.

As I was working with a client one morning, explaining the contents and implications of the chart above, he said, "It's really about courage." He went on to point out to me that when one is unemployed or unhappy at work, one may jump into the first thing that comes along, the first opportunity, trying all the while to reconcile aspects of the new position that don't meet our criteria.

His point was that we should have the *courage to hold fast to our values and criteria* and not just drop into the first suboptimal position that comes along, from which we will soon want to extricate ourselves.

Values

Parallel and closely related to our attributes are our values. Yes, you have values, we all do. This is our religion—the way we see the world.

It is important to model your values in your work as well as in your personal life. Career decisions should be based on some personal, deeply held view of the world.

- Get in touch with your values, those principles you hold dear.
- Discuss your values with a trusted advisor.
- Make a brief list of your values and validate each.
- With values in hand, look at *environments* first—the types of businesses you may/may not want to work in, not companies. For example, the insurance industry, the construction industry, commercial real estate, health care, hospitality, etc., are environments.
- After you have decided what environments you may want to work in, for example: banking or corporate law or higher education, then

  o you can learn about companies within those environments—

    ▪ their cultures,
    ▪ stated values, and
    ▪ policies.

- It's also important to know what you *don't* want—so be prepared to discard whole:

  o environments,
  o industries, and
  o companies.

Find something you love to do, and you'll never have to work a day
in your life!
—Harvey McKay, author

Who Are You?

We have been discussing skills, experience, desired environments, and even values. It's very important to understand and catalogue those items about yourself before embarking on a job search. But there is something even more fundamental, without which your efforts will be misdirected and counterproductive. That something is the self—the professional self. Here's but one illustration.

Belinda Borallo* had been working for twenty-one years as an information technology global director at a Fortune 500 company. She had been putting in twelve to fourteen hours each day, plus being on call nights and weekends. Since her position was global in scope, Belinda had to accept and return phone calls at all hours, day and night, from the opposite side of the world. She had not taken a vacation in all those years.

We met at a restaurant in Miami together with her two best friends, Peggy and Elizabeth. I started an informal CC-101 discussion with her, and I asked her to tell me about herself. She told me about her birthplace, Costa Rica, her loyalty to her current company, her family, even her dog. So I asked,

> *Okay, Belinda, that's all fine, but frankly it's not very relevant to a potential employer. So what can you tell me about your professional self?*

Her two friends agreed with me and encouraged her to discuss her values, motives, her perspectives. She then continued with how she was very loyal to her family, friends, and current employer and how hard her parents had struggled to provide for the family and how hard she had worked to gain a master's degree, etc.

I tried one more time.

> *Belinda, you have skills, experience, and attributes, personal characteristics. Let's start there, with the attributes. Tell me about yourself, the kind of person you are.*

She then told us about her employer's business processes, why some IT infrastructures worked and others didn't, how much she knew about each, and so on.

So I interrupted her softly; I touched her hand and asked,

> *Belinda, who are you?*

Her two friends laughed in sympathy.

She didn't know.
I said,

> *Well, I usually don't go to this level of psychological inquiry in Career Coaching 101, but I feel we must, if you are to make any progress. Belinda, it appears to me that you have been working so very hard for your current employer, over such a long time that although you know your personal work history, you have not had time for introspection. You have not really examined yourself, and you appear unable to answer questions about your core beliefs, your persona, your perspectives, your values and life experiences, other than those that manifest themselves at work. I'm not saying this to you in judgment. It is said with all the love and care that one can convey in a situation like this. Belinda, this is a golden opportunity to define yourself at your core. Think about it. You don't owe me an answer. I just ask that you go off and discuss this with your trusted advisors. Let me know on another day, if you'd like to explore this any further.*

Belinda and I continued the conversation in the restaurant, and she mentioned that she was thinking about putting down $100,000 for a franchise business opportunity. The hair stood up on the back of my neck. I said,

> *Belinda, just a few minutes ago we were discussing the fact that you have not had an introspective moment in over twenty years, and now you're giving serious thought to writing a check for $100,000 for a franchise, even though you don't know if you have the attributes for managing a high-pressure business. The problems of running a business are daunting, even for an experienced entrepreneur. Please, surround yourself with people you trust and discuss who you are, not the pros and cons of a franchise. You're not there yet. You will know when you're ready for that.*

Peggy and Elizabeth emphatically agreed.

Belinda then said that she had been approached by another company, which asked if she would consider doing some process improvement work for them. Now, that sounded much better, if only because there was no capital required.

I had learned a number of things about Belinda in a few hours of conversation, and I had the advantage of her two friends who were very helpful. The way we left it was that she would consider a consulting assignment for business process improvement.

Belinda and I circled back and continued with CC-101 by telephone and e-mail. As of this edition, Belinda was pursuing two opportunities. The one she was interested in was at a technology enterprise with headquarters in Miami. She has had five interviews with top managers, including their chief financial officer. She expects an offer from them. Belinda was also considered by a beverage company based in Atlanta. She interviewed with their chief talent officer and is set to return to meet other members of the management team. Both positions have similar breadth and scope, and she would not be adverse to relocation.

Some weeks later, in an e-mail from Belinda, she informed me that as a result of our conversation on that evening at the restaurant in Miami, she had learned about herself. She wrote that she was now cognizant that her answers revealed that she had not dedicated sufficient time to important things in her life. As a result of our conversation and after reading the draft of this book, she now understands that she has to improve in this respect. She then proceeded to provide examples of the steps she had taken.

By the way, Belinda mentioned that she prepared for those interviews by employing the concepts and T-chart for interviewing, outlined in CC-103—Interviews, and that she found them to be very valuable.

The main point of this anecdote is to underline the need for self-assessment, for introspection and understanding of self *prior* to even a review of the resume.

A resume built on job aspirations alone is a house built on sand. Before reviewing job search tools like the cover letter and resume, you must have a thorough understanding of self, at least of those aspects that affect your professional life. By doing so, you are building a platform for yourself, a platform made up of your values, attributes, and personal characteristics that will—more than anything else—be predictive of your professional success.

On the Importance of Attributes

Attribute: noun, a characteristic or quality of a person or thing, *Webster's New World College Dictionary.*

How do Attributes Make a Difference?

Suppose that Danny Wegman (who owns the renowned chain of supermarkets—Wegmans) needs to hire a pharmacist for one of his seventy supermarkets. He puts a help wanted ad in the newspaper and about ten pharmacists come forward. How will Danny decide from among them?

- All of them are qualified, e.g., by definition, a pharmacist is a credentialed "closed" professional with a license and documented skill set.
- Let's assume that all of the candidates love their work, more or less.
- Let's assume also that they are similarly well situated, vis-a-vis their skills and overall work experience.
- No one clearly stands out above the others in these categories.
- All of them, therefore, have what I call competent resumes. How will Danny Wegman make a choice?

Have you heard hiring managers say, "I hired Denise on instinct?" Or, "There was good chemistry between us, so that's why I chose Greg?" Or, "After looking at everyone's skills and experience, my gut told me that Elizabeth was the right person for the job?"

What are they talking about? What do they mean by instinct? Gut? Chemistry?

They are referring to *attributes*—the candidate's personal attributes. That is, whether the person seems to be compassionate, enthusiastic, detail-minded, extroverted, organized, shy, pugnacious, etc. (see a partial list of attributes in the appendix).

We all unconsciously look for certain attributes when we meet people. In hiring situations, whether we realize it or not, we try to discern those attributes that we think are commensurate with ours even if we can't articulate what they are.

Your attributes, not your skills, are the best predictors of your success. Even the best qualified applicant, in terms of skills and experience, can fail if their attributes are not a match for the employer's stated requirements. That's why it is so important that you understand who you are and demonstrate your personal attributes.

The best recruiters or hiring managers are adept at finding those attributes that are needed in any given hiring situation, and they use their interviewing and screening experience to bring them out in the candidate.

This recent article by a professional services newsletter supports my hypothesis, e.g., that personal attributes—not skills—are critical to your success in a new position:

WHY NEW HIRES FAIL. According to a study by Leadership IQ, 46 percent of newly hired employees will fail within eighteen months while only 19 percent will achieve unequivocal success. But contrary to popular belief, **technical skills are not the primary reason why new hires fail** [author's emphasis]; instead, poor interpersonal skills dominate the list, flaws which many of their managers admit were overlooked during the interview process. The study found that 26 percent of new hires fail because they can't accept feedback, 23 percent because they're unable to understand and manage emotions, 17 percent because they lack the necessary motivation to excel, 15 percent because they have the wrong temperament for the job, and only 11 percent because they lack the necessary technical skills. Eighty-two percent of managers reported that in hindsight, their interview process with these employees elicited subtle clues that they would be headed for trouble. But during the interviews, managers were too focused on other issues, too pressed for time, or lacked confidence in their interviewing abilities to heed the warning signs. "The typical interview process fixates on ensuring that new hires are technically competent," explains Mr. Mark Murphy, chief executive officer of Leadership IQ. "But coachability, emotional intelligence, motivation and temperament are much more predictive of a new hire's success or failure."

In addition, this study found no significant difference in failure rates across different interviewing approaches (e.g., behavioral, chronological, case study, etc.). However, 812 managers experienced significantly more hiring success than their peers. What differentiated their interviewing approach was their emphasis on interpersonal and motivational issues. "Highly perceptive and psychologically-savvy interviewers can assess employees' likely performance on all of these issues," explains Mr. Murphy. "But the majority of managers lack both the training to accurately read and assess candidates, and the confidence to act even when their assessments are correct. Hiring failures can be prevented," he notes. "If managers focus more of their interviewing energy on candidates' coachability, emotional intelligence, motivation and temperament, they will see vast improvements in their hiring success. Technical competence remains the most popular subject of interviews because it's easy to assess. But while technical competence is easy to assess, it's a lousy predictor of whether a newly-hired employee will succeed or fail."

Reprinted with permission from: MICHAEL D. ZINN & ASSOCIATES, INC. ®, Executive Search Newsletter, February 2006.

The best predictors of your professional success are understanding yourself and demonstrating the required attributes for your desired position.

Further evidence to the importance of attributes is in research conducted by Fali Huang and Peter Cappelli, of the National Bureau of Economic Research. Their findings indicate that when employers screen applicants for the attribute work ethic, they realize greater productivity in work teams. In fact, *screening for work ethic as an attribute* in their study was found to be much more effective in attracting and retaining talented staff than screening for cognitive abilities, which does not produce these positive productivity results.

One of my clients reacted this way about the importance of attributes:

For the first time in many years I feel lifted up and, for the lack of a better word, understood. You are the first person to tell me not to restrict my personal attributes (likes and dislikes) in order to find a job, but rather build upon them. For so many years I felt that I had to conform and adjust attributes of myself to conform to some organization. For the first time I feel it is okay to go out for what I love to do, instead of finding something that I can do. I have lost so much confidence in myself, I was without direction, and felt lacking in so many departments, simply because I bought into the idea that I had to fit myself to a job—instead of finding a good match. Now, looking back, I realize that the jobs I loved most were those for which my personality/attributes were well suited, and in which I had established a good rapport with the interviewers/future supervisors almost instantaneously.

It is like you opened my eyes. I know I have a ways to go, but that is okay. Leaving this morning's meeting with you, I felt motivated, energized, and most of all, hopeful. I know it seems exaggerated to have such a reaction to a one-hour-long meeting, but that's how I feel. Thank you so much! I am truly looking forward to working with you on me.

Gabriele Vogt, from her e-mail after our first meeting

Now, back to Danny Wegman and his search for a pharmacist. A smart hiring manager will make his or her final decision, discerning from among qualified candidates, on the *attributes* of the candidate, that is, on the candidate's demonstrated personal characteristics and how well they match the professed requirements of the hiring manager.

What follows is a story of how attributes, when properly positioned, can dramatically affect the outcome of a job search.

Tara Whitman's Story

One of my clients, we'll call her Tara Whitman,* telephoned me and asked for help with her resume. Typically, that's how the conversation starts. "I'm looking for work and I need some help with my resume." This can be done. That is, I can help someone with their resume and send them on their way.

But this is only a fraction of the process. Indeed, the resume is a tool—just a tool. The purpose and tactics of resume writing are detailed in Career Coaching 102 (CC-102). But let's come back to Tara, and how the attributes mentioned in the first part of her resume made all the difference in how she was perceived by the hiring manager and the position she was offered.

Tara started out with a resume that contained all the skills and experience of an accounting clerk, a nonexempt, experienced, business clerical employee. Tara's original resume shows that her objective was "bookkeeper, billing clerk/ collections, accounting clerk, database/Web site administrator, presentations." In my first meeting with Tara to discuss her occupational situation, I saw that she could quickly have landed a position as an accounting clerk. There is a good job market for those skills. But her pay would have been in the low twenties per year at about $10 to $12 per hour. Tara needed a better paying job in order to meet her family's financial requirements. I pointed out to Tara that she had more going on for her than her resume indicated.

During our meeting, I recorded the personal attributes that Tara mentioned about herself. I tested these to make sure she could back them up. So for example, when she said she was results driven, I asked for stories and examples of her work which would support her claim. I asked her for instances of how she had demonstrated attention to detail, and how she had been resourceful.

It's very important, indeed critical, that when you write down an attribute, you are able to back it up. There's no point in feigning to be sociable and outgoing when, in fact, you prefer to work alone and not have your day interrupted by people.

The results of our discussion became evident in her revised resume, where Tara indicated that she is a "results-driven, detail-oriented, enthusiastic office management professional desiring an opportunity to utilize my skills, experience, and attributes to help generate revenue and maintain customer relationships, contract administration, and process optimization for a professional services organization."

In this new "elevator speech" from Tara, where is the bookkeeper? Where is the accounts receivable clerk? She now had a much more potent resume and cover letter, yet her skills and experience were the same, just presented in a more compelling fashion with a greater emphasis on her attributes.

Tara submitted her cover letter and resume (more on the use of attributes in cover letters in CC-102), and she interviewed for a contract administrator position. This would have been a nonexempt position paying in the high $20s. But after the interview process was over, the blue chip company offered Tara a supervisory position, paying $55,000 a year. This was beyond Tara's wildest dreams.

What made the difference? It was positioning Tara in a way that her attributes—results-driven, problem solving, resourceful office management professional—would be in plain view to the hiring manager and would distinguish her from the many other competent but undistinguished resumes that the hiring manager had seen.

Soft Skills? What Soft Skills?

I guess I take umbrage at the notion that personal attributes and interpersonal skills are generally referred to as soft skills. I would dare anyone to say to Tara Whitman that her determination, resourcefulness, tenacity and results-driven nature are soft skills. She would take issue with that, I would bet. And anyone who has had to learn to be more assertive or to become mellower or more detailed or more strategic would tell you that there is nothing soft or easy about learning and honing those characteristics. They are as difficult to master as any "hard" skill, such as writing software or studying for certified public accountant boards. Granted, they can be characterized as interpersonal skills as different from, say, clinical skills or musical skills, but referring to them as soft creates a delusion that they are somehow less important, if not irrelevant—which is definitely a counterproductive notion.

Corporate recruiters will emphasize interpersonal skills including leadership and teamwork. Alan Breznick, of Cornell University, asserts in the university's Cornell Enterprise Johnson School of Business Magazine that "such intrinsic qualities as leadership and teamwork are difficult if not impossible to teach on the job." Recruiters must find a way to elicit these qualities from the candidates through the job interviews.

Karin Ash, director of Cornell's Johnson School Career Management Center says, "Recruiters want candidates who can clearly articulate who they are, where they're going, and who can persuade other people around them."

From Tears to Cheers in Just Five Weeks

> *The only way to do great work is to love what you do.*
> *If you haven't found it yet, keep looking.*
> *Don't settle.*
> —Steve Jobs

Darlene VanSant* knocked on my office door:

Luis, do you have a minute?

Sure, Darlene, come on in, have a seat. What's up?

Luis, my manager just gave me my annual performance appraisal, and, well, I've never received such a low appraisal. I am totally distraught. I did everything he asked me to do. He is so difficult to work for. And after all that, after all the nights and weekends during Christmas and New Years, he gives me a low evaluation! Now I can't even transfer out because they'll see this appraisal and they won't want me. I'm stuck! Right at the peak of my career—I'm stuck with a manager who doesn't like me!

Darlene was in tears by now. I had observed her over the previous several weeks as she worked long hours during the holidays; she never smiled much. She seemed to be always under a lot of pressure. It did not surprise me that she was having a rough time, but now her manager had made it official—in her personnel documents.

> *What can I do, Luis? I'm forty-six, and I've been working my way up the corporate structure. I accepted this assignment in December, as a stepping stone, and now I've hit a rock. I don't know where to go from here. I can't believe this is happening.*
>
> *Darlene, let's set aside an hour to discuss your work history, your aspirations, your aptitudes. I do career coaching, I can help people in situations like yours.*
>
> *You mean, you can work on my resume and stuff like that?*
>
> *Well, yes, eventually we will get to work on and revise your resume. But you've brought a larger problem to the table here, a problem that requires a lot more than a better resume. So let's get together, and I'll explain my process, and we can go one step at time.*

Darlene and I met during the week. After we wrote down what she loved to do and compared it to her resume, it became obvious to her that she did not like what she was doing. That's when I saw the "Christmas tree" light up. This Christmas-tree effect is how I describe the reaction of my clients, which is virtually universal, when they discover that what they love to do is not reflected in their resumes—that is, that they have been working for years doing something they don't like.

In Darlene's case, she was a CPA/MBA. She had been working as an accountant, financial analyst, and now division controller for over twenty years. And in one moment, she discovered that she had been slaving at something she didn't like to do.

> *Darlene, if you don't like accounting and finance, then why did you major in that field, and why did you go on for a CPA plus an MBA?*
>
> *Because I knew I could always get a job.*

Darlene and I met three times. My observation of the situation was that she needed a tactical plan to execute right away, something different to do to get her out of the environment she was in that was crushing her spirit.

She also needed a strategic plan—a long-range plan that would encompass what she loves to do in a productive, financially, and emotionally rewarding way—a plan where she would eventually be able to do exactly what she loved to do.

We listed Darlene's attributes; she wrote her elevator speech and applied it to her resume. In her revised resume, Darlene answered the "So what?" questions. She composed her cover letter and sent it to a manager within the company who had a vacancy in financial analysis.

Darlene was called for interviews. She used the T-chart for interviewing (from CC-103) and was called again for wrap-up. She was offered an internal transfer with a promotional increase. Darlene called me to her office and showed me the offer letter. She said,

> *This can't be true, this can't be right, because I've been in this job less than six months, and they're offering me a promotional increase. There must be a mistake.*

I replied,

> *Darlene, do you see the signatures on this offer letter? They are from the corporate office. This came from Connecticut. This has the highest authority. There's nothing wrong with this offer. Think it over.*

Darlene signed the offer. She started in her new job in only five weeks after she had first come into my office.

She invited me out to lunch to celebrate her promotion. Now, to put this in context, Darlene is a very conservatively dressed, very restrained individual, who measures her words carefully, and is not given to displaying her emotions. While discussing these events over lunch at the restaurant, Darlene looked me in the eye and said,

> *Luis, I was meant to transfer to your building in December. I was meant to meet you. You were meant to be there during the time of my professional crisis. This was meant to happen exactly this way. This was supposed to happen!*

I was surprised at her:

> *Darlene, are you sure you're okay? Why, I've never heard you say things like this. Listen to what you're saying. The things you are saying are very spiritual.*

> *Luis, I'm sure of it, this was meant to happen.*

> *We are not human beings having a spiritual experience; we are spiritual beings having a human experience.*
> —Pierre Teilhard de Chardin

Generating Options

Here are some possible approaches and alternative avenues—use a "blue sky" approach:

- Think about many options.

  o   Ask, "Why?"
  o   Ask, "Why not?"

Potential Obstacles and Workarounds

- Number 1 problem: Are you too hard on yourself?
- Number 2 problem: Do you have unrecognized/unappreciated talent(s)?
- Number 3 problem: Are you settling too quickly, escaping for any quick landing?
- Find the win/win! *You are a solution* looking for their problem(s).
- Align your interests; find common threads, themes among them.

All options are not mutually exclusive—consider options with apparently differing trajectories but aligning varied interests. I have a good friend, Tom Garman, who loves kung fu. He also loves instructing, which is the art of sharing—he loves martial arts, and he loves sharing his knowledge. Tom took his attributes (sharing) and his skills (kung fu), and he set up a successful studio charging a fee for participation.

Someone Will Believe in You

You may at times feel that this whole job search process is not really working, that you don't have the skills, experience, or personal attributes that will support your job search. If your unemployment benefits are about to expire, or if you're running out of time to find work or make a career change, you may feel that there is no escape. Your spouse or significant other becomes weary of your problem. Your options seem scant or nonexistent. It's just you against the world.

- Offload emotion and stress with good friends, family, or trusted advisor.

  o Find a sympathetic, objective observer.
  o Don't overload your spouse or significant other, save them for the big decision.

- Suspend judgment on options (sleep on it).
- Visualize your ideal situation.
- Have faith.

I have been there. I was unemployed for a total of fifteen months in the midnineties. I remember distinctly driving in my old Jeep from Philadelphia to Washington DC for a series of exploratory interviews, and then walking around in my suit and necktie, carrying my briefcase through those streets in Washington, in the sweltering summer heat, saying to myself, "I need to find work. I desperately need to land a job, so I can take care of my wife and three children." Had you been there to see me, you would have seen the willpower in my face, my clenched teeth, and sheer determination. I was going to land, and it had to happen now.

But alas, it was another year before I landed. Lesson learned? *Sheer doggedness and determination alone will be insufficient.* They are required—but insufficient. Muscling through this process may not produce desired results.

Sometimes well-meaning people also miss the mark. I distinctly recall a well-meaning, high-fee career counselor who, while I was unemployed in 1995, asked me to come to his office for his advice and direction. When we met, he looked me very seriously in the eye and said, "Write a letter (to the executive at a company I had targeted)." He continued, "On the envelope, mark it Private and Confidential." He looked so serious, so sincere, he was really convinced that this was the ticket, that this tactic would work to get me the job. But it was the sorriest excuse for career-coaching advice I have ever received. I never went back.

Even if you follow all the suggestions in this book, you may still remain unemployed or unable to make a desired career change *on your timing*. Looking back at my own history, I plotted my job search over the last twenty years and realized that I had been looking for work at precisely those times that the US economy was hobbled by very high unemployment! I not only had all the difficulties faced by anyone looking for work or making a career change; I had faced these vexing issues during eras of national unemployment rates ranging from 5.8 percent to as high as 10.1 percent while hemmed on all sides by fellow baby boomers—all competing for precious few positions.

You may be in dire straights, but there is no need to despair. You will find someone who will believe in you.

You have knowledge, skills, and attributes (KSAs) that someone will want and you can help them solve their business problem. In fact, even if you are lacking some of the skills and experience mentioned in the position profile, you should still be able to demonstrate attributes of importance to the hiring manager and thereby succeed in landing a good job.

Here are some stories of people who believed in me, and how they changed my professional life.

Porter S. Rickley

Mr. Rickley was the regional director of the US Census Bureau, Philadelphia Region, when I was in my late twenties. I had been hired to do community advocacy for the national census that would take place in 1980. After a few months in the job, I was asked if I would like to change career tracks from community advocacy to program supervision. I agreed to this, but I had to give up my US Civil Service exempt grade 11 and take a $3,000/year pay cut to join supervisors-in-training at grade 7. I started my training, and within a year, I was being promoted again.

It was Mr. Rickley who assigned me to supervise the Current Population Survey (CPS), which is the backbone of the national unemployment statistics program. I was only twenty-nine years old, and thanks to Mr. Rickley, I had been trained for supervision and eventually had responsibility for 142 Census employees in a five-state region.

However, I did not recognize the significance of what Mr. Rickley had done for me until he sent me to Washington DC to attend my first national conference of CPS supervisors. It was then, faced with my counterparts from across the country, that I recognized how much he believed in me—he had assigned me to supervise their most important survey, and all the other managers attending the conference were US Census career veterans with over thirty years' experience.

Samuel R. Huston

Sam was the CEO of Lehigh Valley Hospital, the largest hospital in Pennsylvania. The task that he had been given by the board of directors was to merge two hospitals, which had historically been competitors, into one operating entity. He needed to fill the human resources leadership position. I responded to the search and eventually he offered me the position. Here is where Sam differentiated himself. When he offered me the position, he asked me for my salary expectations. So I told him. Not only did he accept my salary requirements, but he raised me by $10,000. I'll never forget that phone call. Can you imagine how eager I was to start work there?

Sam is a brilliant man. He knew how I would react to getting a raise before I started, and I had every intention of vindicating him, of making him look good for his decision to hire me. But wait, there's more. When I went to our first staff meeting with a conference room full of deans of medicine and clinical chairs and administrative leaders, there I was, the youngest again, a thirty-nine-year-old senior vice president. Sam had walked the plank for me; he believed in me, and as you can imagine, I did not disappoint.

Finding someone who is interested in what you have to offer—it's a lot like looking for love.
—LAM

I hasten to point out that neither Porter Rickley nor Sam Huston had known me previously. They were not my childhood friends or fraternity brothers or golfing buddies. So what was at play? What did they see in me?

I did not know it then, but I know it now. They saw my *attributes*. Of course, there were skills and experience that I could demonstrate. But more importantly, they perceived my competence conveyed by my attributes.

Someone will believe in you.

But First You Have to Believe in Yourself!

Stay hungry, stay foolish
—Stewart Brand, *The Whole Earth Catalog*

Donna Highsmith* had graduated from Fairport High School, near Rochester, New York, and earned a bachelor's degree in business administration from the Rochester Institute of Technology. Donna had been referred to me by a mutual friend in the summer of 2003. After doing all the necessary work in CC-101, she secured a position in marketing for a sports trading card company in Rochester. By 2005, she was laid off as a result of a downturn in their business. Donna called me again, and we set up a meeting to revise her paperwork and cast a new strategy. As we entered into a discussion about positions that would be desirable for her, she evidenced a deep longing to leave the cold weather of upstate New York and start a new career and lifestyle in southeast Florida.

Donna was very young but talented and determined. She had set a goal for herself to move to southeast Florida, and all she needed now was a strategy and some tactics. Reviewing her resume, I smiled saying, "This looks like the kind of resume that I have coached." and I had, just a few years before. Donna wanted to find a position in marketing, but she knew that her experience was limited. She decided to first look at a position in sales. I had no doubt, based on my meetings with Donna, that she would be a successful sales representative.

Donna stuffed her Honda Civic with as many earthly possessions as she could carry in it and drove from Rochester to Boca Raton to stay with a friend.

I remember sending her an e-mail as she embarked on her journey to Florida, saying to her, "Donna, I believe in you." This was not empty rhetoric. I knew her as well as one could, and I firmly believed that she would achieve her objective.

Donna found a position as a sales representative with a major copier company. Armed with a steady income, she found her own place to live in Plantation, Florida, and began her career. She kept looking, however, for another job because her base salary was small and the commissions insufficient.

She applied for a position as an internal communications manager for a prominent security company. She had no experience per se in communications, but she was hired at a salary level that she wanted. How did this all take place?

I traveled to Fort Lauderdale and met with Donna for lunch. She was so proud of her accomplishments. I asked her, "Donna, you are so happy that you actually have a glow about you. Tell me, how did you get this job? Tell me about the interviews and what kinds of things they asked you."

As we had lunch, Donna talked to me about her success in landing that dream job. She said, "It was *my attributes*. They saw my energy, my enthusiasm for doing this job. I was told by the hiring manager that the other candidates did not have my attributes."

In addition to her high energy, determination, good personal interactions and being a quick study, Donna also added that other factors were important. We discussed them and came up with a list of five major factors that were in her favor:

- First, her raw intelligence. Donna's IQ is above average, and it shows in how she approaches problems and brings solutions to bear.
- Second, her emotional intelligence. Donna displays an obvious zest for working with the human side of the enterprise, and she successfully navigated the shoals of difficult interviews.
- Third, her mother's influence and counsel. Donna credited her mother with a can-do attitude and generous optimism.
- Fourth, Donna's own life experiences. She had already experienced two layoffs. She wanted a medium-sized company, well established with a sound financial record. She had clarity and was focused on what she wanted.
- And fifth, her spiritual beliefs. Very close to Donna's optimism is a sense that if she listens to the small voice in her heart, she will do well.

What was amazing about Donna was that, mature beyond her young years, she built her plan on a solid foundation—her love for certain aspects of work, her understanding and trust that her attributes would support her, and finally her spirituality—her faith and confidence, which she used to make a decision to drive south, find a pied-à-terre, and begin a new life.

Donna had all those characteristics present when we first met. The work that I did was to hold up mirrors for Donna to see herself. What we did together was to bring out those positive characteristics, those attributes of hers and put them on the table. We examined them objectively and built a resume, cover letters, and an interviewing strategy using my process in such a way that it would afford a hiring manager a good look at them—to Donna's eventual success.

A client writes in her e-mail after our first meeting.

> *I liked the approach of the initial meeting because it was very packaged, simple to understand, and it makes the process appear much less intimidating. This approach would be especially attractive to those individuals who have been in long-term jobs and/or who really don't have a clear idea of what the next steps are. Also, for people like me who are just ready to go get to the next step and move forward!*

> *As an action-oriented person, I liked the direct approach without a lot of fluff. It helps to focus the client on what to do next and forces them to start thinking through the written pieces that will represent themselves (cover letter/resume).*
>
> *Nancy Poisson, Professional Recruiter*

Chapter Summary

The purpose of this section has been to encourage you to connect with your professional values and aspirations—without constraints. Understanding your attributes is critically important to ascertaining your ideal position.

- Think about those things that you have *truly enjoyed*, that make you smile as you write them.
- *Do not constrain yourself* at this point! Do not say, "Well, I love to paint water colors, but there's no money in it." It's critical for you to understand why you love to paint or make cabinets or sell cosmetics or referee boxing or arrange flowers or fight fires. So write it down—what you love to do, and why you love to do it, no matter what it is.
- Be precise, specific on your interests. It's vital to identify what it is that moves you to do those things you love to do.
- Think deeply about why you love to do this activity—and the reason is often beyond the obvious. For example, one client said she really loved fashion design. So we explored this, and in her case it was not about dressing mannequins. What we discovered while discussing this activity is that she really loves sharing with others her interest in helping men to be well dressed, choosing among many options for clothes and accessories. She also helps men with etiquette and social graces to assist them as they socialize among affluent people who can

actually afford her consulting services. This is a lot more than fashion design.

- Ask yourself "Why?" as in why you like participating in those activities—*the specific reasons you love doing certain things.* This can't be emphasized enough.
- Ask yourself "Why not?" for other activities that you have considered but not attempted.
- Look for opportunities to align differing interests with your professional choice, or use them as a platform for a personal business or service.
- In general, you will open your job search conversation with your skills and experience, and you will close it with your attributes.

Your passion drives personal freedom and success!
—Samantha Tassone, President, Human Capital Management

Homework

1. Read this entire book draft.
2. Using the template in attachment A, list those activities within jobs that you love to do. Refer to the instructions at the beginning of this chapter. *It's critical that you write complete sentences,* explaining all your reasons, as if you're writing a letter to a friend describing those things you just love to do. Do not just write one-word answers like "Accounting" or "Selling." You have to write a complete sentence, explaining *why* you like doing that activity—what do you get out of it? What do you like about the results?
3. List all your skills in attachment A. Skills are those things that you've learned, and that you can teach others, like playing piano, litigation, merchandising, designing Web sites, supervising, customer relationship management, etc.
4. List your attributes in attachment A. There is a list of attributes in the appendix. Circle all those that apply. Then number your top five attributes, numbering them from 1 to 5, with number 1 being the highest order and number 5 the least but still very important to you.
5. Now, take out your current resume and underline in your resume all those words that appear in your list of things that you love to do. For example, if you love teaching/educating/instructing, then underline those words, but only if they appear in your resume.

6. After underlining things you love to do in your resume, take a look. What do you think? Did you underline many words? Very few? What's your overall impression? Is there sufficient overlap between what you say you love to do and what you've been doing at your different jobs? Is there a large gap? *How do you feel about this comparison?*

This brings us to the end of Career Coaching 101—how you make it happen!

Brilliant!

—Michael Van Ingen, Cornell graduate, on the simplicity of this
process

TWO

CAREER COACHING 102—The Tool Kit

The Elevator Speech

We begin with the "elevator speech" because this is manifestation of your professional identity. It is your defining label—who you are professionally. Why do we call it an elevator speech? Because it's the carefully packaged answer you would give to the question: "Tell me about yourself." This could really happen. That is, you could find yourself in an elevator with an executive or person with the authority to hire you, or to promote you, and have need of an elevator speech.

Sounds far-fetched? Here is a true story: I was working in Philadelphia at the headquarters of Hay Associates, a prominent management consulting company. One morning, I stepped into the elevator to go up to my office on the fourth floor. A very well-dressed gentleman also stepped in. He was dressed all in black, wearing a bowler hat and carrying a very impressive black umbrella. The gentleman was none other than Dr. Milton L. Rock, who had just arrived from London. He was the managing principal of the company at the time. A very quick exchange ensued between us, and when he asked what I was doing for his company, I used my elevator speech.

What's the point? The point is that, whatever your profession—plumber, nurse, vice president for sales, heavy equipment operator, real estate agent—you should have at the tip of your tongue a brief synopsis of your KSAs: knowledge, skills, and attributes.

What's that you say? The scenario I described is unlikely to happen to you? In fact, there may not even be any elevators in the town where you live and work! Obviously, elevators are not the reason for crafting an elevator speech.

The real reason is to get you to think hard about who you are, professionally, and for you to define it concisely, yet completely and compellingly, for the right opportunity.

The way I approach life is that everyone I encounter is deserving of my attention and respect. Maybe you just can't greet everyone you see on your way to the subway. But certainly you can greet someone at the bus stop or at the gym or at the Little League baseball game. Is an elevator speech appropriate at those times? Of course not. But if conversation develops and you are looking for another opportunity, you may want to carefully explore if that person may be in the position to connect you with someone or some opportunity. In other words, every conversation has the potential of becoming an informal job interview.

Please see attachment B for some examples of actual elevator speeches used by some of my clients. Notice that an elevator speech can be used by a twenty-year-old college student looking for summer work, as well as by a seasoned executive with thirty years experience. Notice also that it works in all arenas—engineering, arts, finance, automotive repair, nursing, and marketing—any endeavor.

How do you build an elevator speech? You begin by listing your attributes. These are one-word labels that describe you. There are no right or wrong attributes. Sociable is just as valuable as shy. Followers are always needed, not just leaders. Detail-minded people are just as important as those with the big picture in mind. The most important aspect of this list is that each attribute be true about you.

Work with someone you trust, or with a professional recruiter, and develop a list of questions that will help you decide on those attributes that you think make you successful at what you love to do. You can ask your trusted advisor to help with this list or ask your significant other or any person that you believe will give you an unvarnished answer.

Jot down all the attributes that come to mind on the list in attachment A, bottom right hand corner of the page. Test them with people you trust. Take a look a the long list of attributes in the appendix. Circle as many as apply to you.

Then choose the top five that describe you. Rank order them from first to fifth. You may have circled twelve or fifteen of them or twenty-seven or thrity-two, but now you have to make some choices. The objective is to narrow them down to those attributes that (a) are true about you and (b) may interest an employer.

For example, you may say punctual, productive, mature, all of which are interesting to a hiring manager. You could also be romantic or spiritual, but an employer is probably not interested in those.

Having narrowed down the list to about five, it's time to construct a sentence that describes who you are, professionally. Take a look at some examples in attachment B.

The elevator speech is like a run-on sentence containing a number of key words that the interviewer can use to start or continue a conversation about you (more on how to use the elevator speech in CC-103—Interviews). Some of the key words you will use in your elevator speech are attributes; others are skills or experience. For example, career wise you probably want to be known as a "commodity purchasing professional" or "tool crib coordinator" or "network analyst" or "retail floor supervisor" or whatever your current occupational circumstances. The skills, knowledge, and attributes that you pack around your elevator speech will lend substance and credibility.

Try your hand and draft an elevator speech. Begin by jotting down some attributes. Then try to build a sentence around them. Some people have a lot of difficulty with this. I often hear from clients that it is for them the hardest part of this preparation process. They say, "I don't know what to say about myself."

Begin with a simple draft, a short sentence about yourself. Then explain the process to someone you trust and try it out on a number of people. Ask them, after they heard your elevator speech, what words they remember. What attributes or skills would they want to pursue in conversation with you if they were a hiring manager?

The Objective

Many candidates are taught by well-meaning coaches that they should begin their resume with their objective statement. Typically, the objective on their resumes reads, "Seeking challenging position where I can use my education, skills, and experience for growth and opportunity in a dynamic organization."

What's wrong with that? Seems reasonable. Unfortunately, it fails on many fronts.

First, it reads just like everyone else's objective. Second, it only says what the candidate wants (which presumes that the hiring manager is charitably interested). Third, the reader has just read the first paragraph but still doesn't know anything about the candidate. So frankly, it's a perfectly useless statement when redacted that way.

By contrast, with an elevator speech, the reader is informed about *what the candidate has to offer,* which is distinguishably different from that of others. The elevator speech at the top of the resume gives you, the candidate, a "face." The elevator speech begins to sketch out what kind of person you are.

The rest of the resume will be packed with information about your education, experience, skills, duties, and accomplishments; but it's the elevator speech in combination with your cover letter that defines you as a person for the reader. And in the end, my friend, when you are a finalist among two or three, it's w*ho you are* that will make the difference.

The Resume

The purpose of a resume is to get a job, right?

No.

The purpose of a resume is to get the first interview.

Employers use resumes for a number of reasons. An obvious one is to learn about your skills, experience, and attributes as outlined in the resume. This is a screening activity, where the recruiter or hiring manager basically separates or rank orders the candidates from apparent best to nonqualified. If the resume is of interest to the employer, s/he will use it to generate some questions for your interview. The resume is also the first glimpse the employer will have of your abilities to write (grammar, spelling, syntax, consistency, brevity, clarity, etc.). You must pay attention to detail, organize your thoughts, categorize your information, and communicate your message.

Let's revisit the story of Tara Whitman, mentioned in chapter 1. First, we discussed what she loves to do—project management, contract administration, customer relationship management, process optimization, office operations, administrative logistics, research and problem solving. Notice that she did not mention, when building the list of what she loves to do, anything about love for payables or a passion for receivables, databases, or ledgers. Tara and I then discussed how to build her resume so that her attributes would be demonstrated in the results and accomplishments of her work experience.

Competent Resumes versus Passionate Correspondence

Many resumes that cross my desk are poorly thought out, not well organized, inconsistent in style and format. The better resumes are what I call "competent"—that is, they are fairly well designed, consistent in style and format, and they do a fairly good job of describing where the applicant has worked, their duties and responsibilities, the scope and reach of their charter as well as listing some of their accomplishments.

The problem is that even the competent resumes are lacking information about *how well* the applicant has done their job. So even the competent resumes read like a very long job description.

When discussing this problem with some of my clients, they often reply,

> *Well, I'll tell them how well I performed in those jobs when I'm in the interview.*

Can you picture in your mind my wry smile? My response is,

> *And why do you believe you'll get an interview, given that your resume reads like a two-page job description, and you have not even once demonstrated with facts or figures how well you did your job? How is the reader to know that you are quicker, better and faster than the person you would replace?*

Answering the "So What?" Question

Summarizing, once you've organized your chronological resume into a competent resume, the easiest part is done.

The difficult part, as many of my clients tell me, is answering the "so what?" question. This means thinking about those things you've done very well, and then specifically demonstrating it. For example, if you write,

"Responsible for sales of building supplies in New York, New Jersey and Connecticut."

So what? All that tells the reader is that the applicant was responsible for selling office building hardware in a three-state area. But how well did s/he do it?

Here's how to answer the "so what?" question:

"Responsible for book of business in New York, New Jersey and Connecticut.

- Exceeded sales quota by 21 percent over previous year.
- Reduced customer complaints by 43 percent.

- Improved sales to delivery times by 12 percent.
- Received several memos from management praising my performance.
- Finished the year at third highest among seventeen representatives."

Some would argue that I picked an easy example, a sales career, where everything is easily measured. And that's true. The sad fact is that some sales professionals fail to point out their own metrics on their resumes.

Admittedly, the challenge is to objectively look at the work you're doing and measure it quantitatively and qualitatively to demonstrate how well you've done.

Whether your career choice is easily quantifiable and readily yields metrics—or not—you still have to find ways to measure and quantify *the value of your contribution*. This can be done in any career.

If you cannot measure the value of what you do, then you can rest assured that you are not the only one who notices. Your manager and your peers and subordinates will know that what you're doing can either be done better by someone else or discarded or outsourced. So measure your value you must!

Measuring the Value of Your Contribution

One of my clients Beverlie was a professional harp player, piano player, and teacher. Beverlie had been sending out her resume to many school districts but was not getting any responses. Upon reading her resume, everyone agreed it was a competent resume. The problem was that the school districts were receiving many resumes as good as hers. There was little in her resume that distinguished it from those of many others. I asked her,

> *Beverlie, are you a good music teacher?*

> *Oh yes, of course I am.*

> *Okay, but from reading your resume, how do I know that you're really good?*

Beverlie lit up like a Christmas tree:

> *Well, you should see what the parents say, what the students say about me. I get letters, commendations. I get many compliments for playing*

my harp at weddings. I've been told by some students and parents that I'm the best music teacher they've ever had!

Beverlie's eyes were now as big as saucers as she related her achievements to me. Her face demonstrated the passion that she had for playing the harp and for teaching music. I had no doubt that she is as good as she said she was. The challenge for her was to demonstrate in her resume and cover letter that she was far above average, that she was an *excellent, an extraordinary* piano and harp teacher.

Beverlie, you've convinced me that you are really passionate about playing the harp and teaching music. But I don't see that in your cover letter or in your resume.

Oh, but you can't say things like that in a cover letter or on a resume.

Why not?

Well, you just don't. It's not professional.

The Cover Letter

Beverlie was functioning under the assumption that demonstrating one's passion and love for one's chosen career was not really professional. If she would do it at all, she related, she would only do it during an interview, face-to-face. However, even then she confessed she would have been guarded, reticent, careful with her words—in other words, professional.

Where is your passion? If you are going to spend a significant portion of your week in some work activities, wouldn't you want those activities to at least have some measure of love or passion in your life? I hope your answer would be "yes" to that question. How do you convey your love, your passion, for certain work activities?

You do so via the cover letter.

The cover letter is brief and to the point. It's only one page. And it only has three paragraphs. The three paragraphs are as follows:

a. Use an emotional hook in your first paragraph.
b. Include the words *love* and *passion* in your second paragraph.

c.   Mention three to five attributes in your third and last paragraph with a note that you'll be calling to follow up.

The Emotional Hook

The best way to start a cover letter is to be able to say, in the first sentence of your first paragraph, something along these lines:

> "I was referred to your office by (name of someone known to the person to whom you're writing)."

Or,

> "We have a friend in common—(person's name) tells me that he is part of your organization."

Or,

> "I was in temple last Friday, and I learned that (person's name) sees you regularly at your daughter's soccer games."

This approach sets what I call "the emotional hook." The recipient knows immediately that there is a second-degree connection between the two of you. This is the best way to establish a personal connection, only two degrees apart from your target audience. This reassures her/him because it provides a built-in reference source *even before they've read your resume!*

Since this is the preferred approach, using a second-degree connection, then the best way, indeed the only way, for you to build a vast database of second-degree connections is to *go out and begin networking.*

Conversely, the worst approach begins this way: "I am responding to your Help Wanted advertisement."

If this approach is the only one available, then by all means use it. But the best approach is to establish a second-degree connection in the first sentence of your letter. And to do that, you must begin your networking. More specifics about strategies and tactics for networking are found later in this chapter.

The "Love" Word and the "Passion" Word

Pardon my passion.
—LAM

You might think: "Wait, isn't that kind of corny and not really "professional," using those words—*love* and *passion*—in work-related correspondence?"

Clients like Beverlie are very hesitant to use this word in their job search correspondence. They tell me that they've never seen that before, that it would not look professional. I understand their hesitancy, but there is more than one approach.

The straightforward approach is simply to say something like:

> "While I was at KPMG, I loved meeting new customers and learning their requirements."

Or,

> "Throughout my seven years with Kraft, I demonstrated my passion for product quality."

Surely that wasn't so hard. Actually, maybe you didn't even notice that I used the love word and the passion word.

But there is another way, besides using first person singular. That's the convenience of third-person singular, as in this example:

> "My manager wrote in my performance appraisal that my love for statistical analysis is demonstrable."

Or,

> "Several customers attested to my passion for following up to ensure complete customer satisfaction."

In these examples the love and passion words are used to describe the writer—you, so they are objective in their source—and just as powerful.

The Third and Last Paragraph

To close your brief cover letter you should now give them a little insight into your personal self by appropriately mentioning three of your top attributes, as in,

Perhaps your enterprise can take advantage of my dedication to GAAP in payroll practices, my integrity, and my tenacity in forensics to improve the operations of your payroll department. I will call your office to follow up on [name the date].

Always finish with a note that you will be following up, and then jot it in your calendar so that you close the loop with them. Whether they are receptive to your candidacy or not, it's still information that you need in your campaign.

The Next Best Thing

While you're on the hunt, always, *always* have plan B!

- Sit down and explore the Next Best Thing in case your ideal plan fails to work.
- Even if you are a finalist for three positions—keep looking!

Here's why. In November 1995, just before Thanksgiving, I was a finalist for three positions, all of them as vice president of human resources. My wife and I went to see my career counselor Ted to brief him on my progress. I pointed out to Ted that things were looking good—I was a finalist for three positions.

Ted said,

> *Have you thought about what you will do if you don't get any of them?*
>
> *What do you mean, Ted? I'm a finalist for three big jobs, two in the Washington area and one in New Jersey.*
>
> *Yes, but what if you don't get any of them?*
>
> *Ted, I'm sure I'll get one of them. Probably two. Maybe a clean sweep! Wouldn't that be sweet!*

Yes, that would be sweet. But what's your plan if you don't get any of them?

I didn't have plan B.

And I didn't get any of the three jobs.

What followed from that point was months of frustration and agony. It was November, so everyone turned their attention to their Thanksgiving holiday plans followed by Christmas and New Year's.

During those six to eight weeks, recruiting activities will slow down or stop in many companies. Many organizations have fiscal years ending on December 31. A typical comment around that time is, "Well, we have to finish with a strong bottom line this year, so we're not doing any hiring until next year. We can't even hire replacements for those who have left."

What can be learned from this experience?

Always, always keep looking!

Don't stop interviewing, calling, networking, reaching out to people and sending out correspondence even while you are a finalist for a position.

You must maintain the momentum!

The gestation period of a job search for a good-paying job can be very long, and losing just a few days can set the gestation process back, especially just before holidays.

On the Importance of Meeting People

Networking is like the lottery—you have to play to win.

—LAM

You do *not* know where your next job is coming from.

Maybe you didn't get it.

You do not know where your next job is coming from!

This is why you have to participate in networking. You must be out there meeting and greeting people. You have to be open and yet discerning to many and all possibilities.

It was January 1996, and I had been unemployed for nine months. Part of my networking activities included attending a monthly meeting of unemployed human resources professionals, which was held in Princeton, New Jersey.

During those meetings we would make photocopies of leads and information about jobs that may be opening up and then exchange them. Everyone was supposed to contribute leads—that was the price of admission. The intended result was that everyone would go home with a copy of what everyone else had brought in. Unfortunately, 99 percent of the leads weren't very useful, but it was a start. Remember, there was no Google or Monster or Yahoo then or even reliable e-mail service. Virtually everything was still done in hard copy in those days.

On the day of that January meeting, I woke up early to find about six inches of fresh snow on the ground. My wife said,

Why are you up? Where are you going?

I said,

I'm going to the HR meeting in Princeton.

She said,

Why? It's eighty miles away and look at all that snow. The roads aren't even plowed. Nobody will be there.

I said,

Honey, I have to go. I can't just sit here. Even if only a few people show, I'll have someone to talk to, and that may lead to something. I'll get an early start, so I can take my time.

As I drove through unplowed snow from Pennsylvania to New Jersey, I thought about how frustrated I was. I had no leads. I didn't even know who I was going to call on Monday morning. With everyone coming back to the office from the holidays, it would probably be weeks before I could have my next telephone screen or personal interview. I was desperate.

While driving, I was thinking that I would get to Princeton and find no one there. I had visions of just turning around on the parking lot and driving home empty-handed.

I arrived at the designated place, and the parking lot was full! Incredible. Everyone was there, even with all that snow.

You meet people for a reason, for a season, or for a lifetime.
—Peggy Ann Navajas

Walking into the meeting room, I greeted everyone there as we milled around and exchanged information. Just then Martha, one of the attendees, said to me,

> *Luis, don't you have experience in manufacturing and with labor relations?*

I said,

> *Yes, I do. I have five years of labor negotiations experience in a battery manufacturing company.*

Martha said,

> *I heard that Xerox is looking for someone with your experience.*

That was all.
That was the job lead, in its entirety.
So I thought, "Where is Xerox?"
Remember, I couldn't just run home and jump on Google or Yahoo to find out more about a company. Instead, when I got home I was off to the library to find out more about Xerox by looking in Dunn & Bradstreet, in telephone directories, among annual reports, and in other dusty books and publications.

I found out that Xerox had a large presence in Rochester, New York. "Rochester?" I thought, "Where is Rochester?" Using phone books, I drilled down until I found some phone numbers.

On Monday morning, I started making phone calls. Eventually someone answered the phone. It was Bill Strusz. I have to mention his name because I was so impressed that he actually took my call! Bill was working in Xerox corporate human resources department at the time (he is now retired.) I told him about my work experience, and I answered a few of his questions. He said, "Okay, send me your resume." So I did.

Then silence.
I called to follow up but no response from Xerox.

In April, I received a call from an executive search consultant representing Xerox. She had my resume in her hand and wanted me to fly up to New York and meet with her.

Well, the rest is history. I landed an excellent job in Xerox in Rochester, and my work experience there has been the best ever.

What's the point of that story?

If I had not joined the Princeton Human Resources Network . . .

If I had not introduced myself to Martha earlier and related to her my experience . . .

If I had not driven to that meeting that one day because of the snow . . .

If Martha had not driven to the meeting that day . . .

If Martha had not remembered me . . .

If I had not taken her lead seriously . . .

If I had not researched Xerox . . .

If I had not called and persisted until I got someone on the phone . . .

If I had not sent in my resume . . .

If Bill Strusz had not forwarded my resume to the executive search consultant . . .

Do you see the point? Any break of any link in this long chain would have destroyed my chances. But it started with me *joining a network and going to the meetings!*

By the way, take time to remember and be grateful to those who help you—when I was offered the job in Xerox, I sent a large bouquet of flowers to Martha.

> *I had met Martha for a reason.*

Author Richard Bolles, in his best-selling classic job search book *What Color is Your Parachute?* reports that a job search is more likely to be successful (84 percent) when it is done in a group with other job hunters, applying the most effective strategies. This rate drops by 15 percent when the strategies are followed alone.

Dr. Nathan Azrin, PhD, is one of the job search experts who advanced the notion of job clubs, and replicated studies have proven the success of that formula—networking.

According to Execunet, *http://www.execunet.com*, networking is the primary source for executive search firms for finding candidates. They reported their sources as follows:

- Networking 35 percent
- Online research, excluding job boards 30 percent
- Online job postings 29 percent
- Firm's database/resume files 28 percent
- Advertising 24 percent
- Faculty contacts 24 percent

(Numbers add up to more than 100 percent because a resume can be found in more than one source).

Another phenomenon that is growing rapidly as of this book edition is social networking also referred to as Web 2.0. While college students and recent graduates are very familiar with Facebook and MySpace, more experienced and business-only networkers will appreciate the power of business networks like LinkedIn.

Business networking tools like LinkedIn can be used to conduct searches of people in certain companies or industries or just to track down persons in our work history who may hold the key to a potential opportunity for introduction or advancement.

I encourage you to find out how social networking tools like LinkedIn work. It's free for you and me. Just fill out your profile and reach out to people you know. Some recruiters realize its value, and they pay a fee to take advantage of its powerful search, job posting, and advanced networking capabilities.

> *Ninety percent of success is just showing up*
> —Woody Allen

Remember, for local and regional networking follow Woody Allen's advice: join the group and attend their meetings.

Steps to Lifelong Networking

If you want to know more about networking tactics you can find and read whole books on this topic. I won't replicate their fine work here. But I will leave you with the substance of my experience and the demonstrable accomplishments of those who have effective networking practices.

How do you go about networking? Put this into practice:

- Every person you meet may lead you to your next job.

- *Join* local professional associations and networks.
- *Go* to their meetings and mixers.
- Join digital networks.
- Read professional journals:

  o identify high flyers (accomplished people or up and coming leaders),
  o contact them,
  o try to meet them and discuss your mutual professional interests,
  o ask them about their experiences,
  o and learn from them.

- Volunteer for a professional project—doing research, making phone calls, analyzing data, writing reports, etc.
- Bring value to the networking meeting and reciprocate—be a giver of tips and leads, not just a taker.
- Remember to show gratitude to those who are helping you with tips and networking contacts.
- Send your contacts and networking friends an e-mail from time to time, let them know how you're making progress, and ask them how *they* are doing.
- Make sure you respond to any e-mails or phone calls from networking contacts to express appreciation. That's what *you* would want!
- Keep in touch even when people move out of town. They still know a lot of people where you are. And if they moved to another city to start a new position, it's the right thing to do to show some concern for their well-being.
- Seek to become the best connected person in your career track, e.g., whether it's in marketing, taxation, fashion design, finance, imaging science, bioethics, computer engineering, or whatever your field of work is—seek to become the "go to" person.
- Use discernment, consider the source and circumstances of leads that are given to you but generally *follow up on every lead.*

> *The only statistic you need to know is, how many people do you*
> *know, and how many people know you?*
> —Tracey Aiello, founder, the August Group

Chapter Summary

In this second chapter, you have been provided an outline for construction of essential tools for your job search. Explicit directions have been provided for you so you can build

- an elevator speech, which describes your skills, experience and attributes quickly and effectively;
- your professional objective, stated crisply, with clarity;
- a passionate resume, which depicts those professional activities and personal interests for which you have a passion, and one that answers the "so what?" question; and
- a brief but effective cover letter.

This chapter also emphasized the importance of measuring your value added, measuring your professional contribution. The effectiveness of using the emotional hook was emphasized as an opening sentence in the cover letter to immediately connect with the reader. The importance of using the *love* word and *passion* word was explained with examples. In the instructions for the cover letter, the importance of the third paragraph was explained, wherein you should ask for assistance in expanding your network and indicating that you will be following up.

One crucial tenet of this chapter is the concept that you should always, always keep looking for the next best thing. The critical value of networking was emphasized and examples provided.

Homework

1. Draft an elevator speech using the top five attributes that you think best describe you, and include it in your resume as you make changes. Refer to sample elevator speeches in attachment B.
2. Take a look at the elevator speech that you drafted—make sure your elevator speech uses the top five attributes that you think best describe you. Include this elevator speech at the top of your resume.
3. Go through each accomplishment in your resume and make sure that you answer the "so what?" question at the end of each achievement using facts and figures or even testimonials whenever possible. See sample resume of June Farnsworth, attachment D. Examples:

- "Increased efficiency of manufacturing process yielding 17 percent less defective products and saving $172,000."
- "Responsible for helping customers try on their dresses and outfits in junior department of Macy's. Received four letters of commendation from retail customers."
- "Accountable for problem solving in the field, diagnosing electrical faults and service interruption. Commended by supervisor for efficient, courteous service."
- "Helped attorneys draft their briefs by researching our legal database, enabling them to spend more time strategizing their approach to litigation."

2. Draft a cover letter using the template in attachment C. Pretend you are writing to a target company or hiring manager. Write as if you actually wanted an interview opportunity. Make sure you use an emotional hook in your first paragraph, include the words *love* and *passion* in your second paragraph, and mention three to five attributes in your third and last paragraph.
3. Choose an environment where you think you might want to work. You can research environments using *The Book of Lists* published by business journals in most cities. Make a brief list of those environments where you think you'd like to work and also another list of those places where you know you would *not* like to work.
4. Use an Internet web browser (Yahoo, Google) to search for networking groups. Join at least two groups and *start going to their meetings.*
5. Use these attachments found in the back of the book: cold networking call (attachment F) and warm networking call (attachment G) as necessary to conduct your networking calls.

> *I stuck with your system and utilized the job search tools. Now I have a boss whom I can respect and learn from and our relationship is the type we both wanted—collaborative, a partnership. The work is more meaningful and much better suited. In the first two days, I have been able to make a contribution, to make a difference, make more money, work closer to home, and to work in a beautiful environment. Thank you again!*

> —Sharon Bahringer, from her e-mail after landing a great position

THREE

CAREER COACHING 103—The Interview

Interviews

The purpose of the first interview is to get the job, right?
No.
The purpose of the first interview is to get the second interview.
Don't worry about hitting a home run, just hit a single!
Here's what I mean by that. I used to coach my daughter and her team when she played fast-pitch softball. Alison is not a big girl, and we knew that she had a slim chance or none of hitting the ball hard to the outfield. Alison's strength was that she was a fast runner. So the plan was to get her to first base.

Alison, just bunt or take four balls or even get hit by the pitch! Just get to first base, and you can steal from there.

Sure enough, she would typically bunt or take a walk to first.
With Alison standing on first, I would signal to her: "Go on the first pitch." Everyone knew that Alison would steal second base on the first pitch. She did this for years. There were very few catchers who could catch the pitch, stand up, and throw over the pitcher to second before Alison reached the bag. After stealing second, she would steal third, and eventually advance to home plate.
So using the analogy above, the idea is to focus on the upcoming interview. Prepare thoroughly for it. The objective is to do very well at this point (first base), and thereby increase the chances of advancing to the next interview (second base).

If you have taken care of your homework at the end of CC-101 and CC-102, you are now ready to take interviews. There is no need to stress yourself out. If you do all the appropriate work to prepare, the chances are pretty good that you will be better prepared than the person interviewing you.

What follows is an interviewing strategy, plus some tips and tactics.

Three Tools for the Interview

If you follow the process suggested below, you will be armed with three things that you need for a successful interview.

One: You will have an answer to their first question, which is likely to be, "Tell me about yourself," or "What have you been doing (professionally)?" or even "Why are you here?" Whatever the form of their question, you will be prepared, and they will be impressed with your prompt and concise reply.

Two: You will have a list of all that they want from a candidate. They will be impressed with your anticipation of their concerns and with the quality of your answers to their problems.

Three: You will know what questions to ask them and in what order, so they will be impressed with your analytical skills and sense of process discipline.

To help you with the first interview, these are the questions that you will be asked and, following those, some that you will ask.

One: The First Question That You Will Be Asked

Let's now work on the first question that a recruiter or hiring manager is likely to ask you. The question "Tell me about yourself." can be used by the recruiter or hiring manager as the warm-up question, or after a chat about the weather or your travel experience while getting to the interview.

This question, *no matter what form it takes*, will be asked in the early part of the interview process.

It can take the form of "What adjectives would others use to describe you?" You would use your top five attributes, which are part of your elevator speech, to answer that question.

Another variant could be "What interests you about this job that we posted?" You would tailor your elevator speech, on the fly, toward the position for which you are interviewing. The objective is to hijack the question and answer it in such a way that you effectively set the agenda, describing your skills, experience, and attributes.

Yet another form it could take could be, "I see you have a strong manufacturing background, but how will that help you in our finance and banking organization?" Your elevator speech will have anticipated this potential pushback from the hiring manager, and it would contain key words that will serve to calm their fears.

For example, if they ask, "Why are you interested in the PAETEC company?" you may respond with your elevator speech nested in a natural response, such as,

> *My good friend, Liliana, who works in your customer service department, alerted me that PAETEC was interested in expanding their call center supervisory staff. I am a results-driven, experienced manager with eleven years in the customer service space, employing my compassionate but firm people management skills to lead teams in accomplishing extraordinary things.*

At this point, it's important to pause, let the words sink in and let the recruiter choose what to ask you about—your team leadership, your compassion, your call center technical experience. Even at this early stage of the interview, at the first sentence of the conversation, you've already laid out an agenda—on your terms.

For any variant of this question, when asked early in the interview exchange, you will always have a crisp answer—your elevator speech. This is the same elevator speech that you designed and wrote in CC-102, which you wrote at the top of your resume.

Keep in mind you have to answer the question using the *content* of your elevator speech, sounding natural and smooth in your delivery. Practice this with a trusted advisor. Let them ask you the first question in various forms and learn different ways to answer it while delivering the *content* of the answer. It's critical that the interviewer hear the key words that you are trying to convey—the substance of your message.

Those Pesky Behavioral Interviewing Questions

Some people have heard of behavioral interviewing techniques, and they profess being afraid of them. I frankly don't understand why. The purpose of a behavioral interview question, when properly presented, is to learn how the candidate handled or managed a situation in the past.

A behavioral interview question does not have the word *would* in it, as in "what would you do if . . ." a situation were to arise. The behavioral interview question always looks to the past and asks what you *did* under such and such circumstances. The rationale for asking it this way is that social research shows that people are likely to respond the same way in the future as they have in the past, when similar circumstances are present.

A behavioral interview should be very easy for anyone to answer. The key to the response, indeed, the key to all healthy relationships, is to tell the truth, the unvarnished truth. The employer who properly uses behavioral-based interviewing is trying to assess your fit into the organizational culture and your ability to succeed in the new position.

Here is a sample of some behavioral interview questions, and what to do in preparing your response:

- "Have you been in a situation when you inherited a team of people who were totally demoralized by their previous management? What did you do about it?"
- "The last time that you started a new job, what did you do in the first few days?"
- "Tell me about a time when you saw a colleague cheat on her expense account. What did you do?"
- "Can you tell me about a time when you embarked on a project that turned into a failure? What was it about, and how did you handle it?"
- "Tell us about a time when you had to convince others of your point of view."
- "Have you ever had a manager who was very difficult to work with? Tell me about the circumstances (no names) and how you handled it."

There may be some behavioral interviewing questions that don't link directly to anything in your work history. For example, maybe you've never seen anyone cheating on their expense account, or maybe you have never managed a group of people. In those instances, you can *use your attributes to reply, saying what you would do.* So you could reply saying, "I'm very *respectful* of other people's talents, skills, and integrity; so if I inherited a disillusioned team, I would trust and engage them in such a way that they could each shine in their own area of skill and expertise."

Handling Other Questions That May Arise

This book will not attempt to anticipate every question that an employer may ask. In fact, there are many specialized books dealing with the many questions that may arise accompanied by suggestions for responses. But here is a sampling of the types of inquiries that some hiring managers may want to employ.

Employers may ask questions from any number of perspectives. The following are some questions that an employer may reasonably ask:

- *What are your strengths? What are your weaknesses?*
- *If I asked some people who know you well to describe you, what three words would they use?*
- *What did you love about your most recent position? What did you dislike doing?*
- *What are your goals for the next three, five, ten years?*
- *Why do you want to work in our organization?*
- *How will you achieve your professional objectives in our organization?*
- *Have you read about our new market segmentation strategy? What do you think of it?*
- *What can your next manager do in order to help your career?*
- *In what ways do you think you can make a contribution to our organization?*
- *What is our reputation in the community? What are people saying about our company?*
- *Why did you choose that course of study?*
- *What extracurricular activities have you been involved in? Why those?*
- *Where do you see yourself in five years?* This is not a particularly valuable question, in my view, because nowadays there are positions and even whole industries that did not even exist five years earlier. The question may be suited for traditional, mature industries with very well established structures—finance, manufacturing, not-for-profit management. But this type of question must be handled differently if your work environment is information technology, Internet vending, or computer gaming.

There are whole books devoted to interviewing questions, so we won't try to cover them all in this publication. But, certainly, if you want to ensure that you have thought about many forms of questions that a recruiter may throw at you, or that you could pose to them, I would refer you to many publications and even Web sites, which would be very helpful.

Some Questions You Hope They Don't Ask

Some hiring managers want to play with the candidate, consciously or unconsciously, or to show off or needle the candidate to see a reaction. These questions have no rational purpose, but some insist on asking them, and they are quite proud of how clever they are. Here are some examples:

- *I have very high expectations of you in this interview. Are you going to disappoint me?*
- *How soon after you start will you want my job?*
- *Do you like the Yankees or the Red Sox? Be careful, your answer may seal your destiny!*
- *If you were told to bunny hop down the hall, would you do it? Why? Why not? (I have actually been asked this question!)*
- *Would you rather be a monkey or a zebra, and why?*

Yes, Virginia, those questions, and others that are not fit to print, have actually been asked.

Illegal Questions That Employers Should Never Ask

Let's set the record straight. It is the responsibility of every hiring manager to discriminate.

That's right. Every hiring manager discriminates. They must.

That's the whole purpose of the interview—to discriminate among all the candidates on the basis of legal factors: education, experience, credentials, attributes, and the like.

Employers are *prohibited* from discriminating on the basis of factors deemed illegal, such as race, religion, sex, nationality, marital status, age, physical ability/disability, etc.

The following questions would constitute a violation of federal or state laws concerning terms and conditions of employment if they were asked anytime, from preemployment through employment and even postemployment:

- How old are you?
- What's your nationality?
- Where were your parents born?
- What is your birth date?
- With whom do you live?
- Are you married, divorced, single?
- Are you disabled?
- How many children do you have?
- Who is going to take care of your children while you are at work?
- How much do you weigh?
- When was your last physical exam?
- Have you ever been arrested?

How do you respond to those illegal questions? The fact is that you can go ahead and answer any of them. It's up to you. You do have a few alternatives:

- You can answer the question about where your parents were born, for example, and emphasize that as a result of their many work-related relocations, you have learned to become very adaptable.
- Or you can decline to provide an answer, but doing it in such a way that it doesn't break the relationship you are trying to establish (if indeed it's worth establishing—one thing is to ask an illegal question out of ignorance of regulations, another is out of intent to discriminate, but you have to decide on the spot).
- Or you might want to examine the rationale behind the question, such as if they ask about citizenship because of requirements for a Department of Defense contractor.

Some Exceptions

In some circumstances employers have a responsibility to ensure that certain parameters are met, such as employment contingent on passing a drug test, background check (evaluation of conviction records that pertain to the job in question), US citizenship for national security clearance, gender in the case of male model/female model for merchandising, etc. However, in those instances the employer bears the responsibility and burden that the preemployment requirements are directly tied to the job opportunity.

Two: The Tee Chart—Knowing Their Needs and Educating Your Interviewer about Your Contributions

The second way to prepare for the interview is to write your Tee chart for interviewing. You simply take a piece of paper, write a line down the middle of it, top to bottom. Then a line across the top, about one inch from the top of the page (see attachment E). Then on the top left you write, "What they want" and on the right, "What I can offer or contribute."

Now the real work begins—to understand what they want and concisely write it down as bullets on the left side of the page. You can get this information from their job descriptions and the notes you took during a phone interview. It's also very helpful if you can gather information from insiders.

If you're using your personal computer to do this, write everything you know about the position. This is usually found in the job description or job posting. Identify those desired items in a list, as bullets, in any order. Then go back and prioritize them based on what you know about the company, its mission, your hiring manager's priorities, and any other data points you have.

The objective is to build a roster of all their needs, their problems, their desired skills and experience in an orderly, prioritized list.

Now that you know what they want, bullet by bullet, it's time to write down how you would help them with their problem.

Think about your experience. For each of their requirements (on the left of the T-chart) write down on the right side of the T-chart something you've done, something you have accomplished that fulfills that requirement. It's important here that you are crisp but complete, so that when the item comes up you can readily respond to it with clarity and conciseness.

Actually, to optimize this technique, you should give the T-chart to a trusted advisor so they can quiz you. You should spend about a one-half hour rehearsing questions and answers. This will build quick relationships between their potential questions and your answers. By practicing your answers, they will be right on the tip of your tongue for quick and complete response.

If there is a gap in your knowledge or skills, write down one or two attributes which would help you achieve that level or expertise. For example, you could say, "While my strength is in compensation, not benefits, I am a *collaborative* person who *works well cross functionally* in a *participative style*, so I will seek out the advice and counsel of your resident experts in the benefits area."

Three: The Questions That You Must Ask

You will ask the recruiter at least these three questions, beginning with a large overarching blue sky topic and moving to smaller more immediate topics in the order found below:

- One: "What can you tell me about: this company, its culture, its founder, its recent event that I read about in the news?"

  o Prepare to ask this question by visiting the Web site, understanding a brief history of the company, learning about its founder or current CEO.
  o Try to find recent news events, which are often found in their Web site.
  o Be cognizant of the company's products and services, recent acquisitions, thrusts in new market directions, major competitors, and research breakthroughs.
  o Study the company's reach and scope—is it local, regional, national, multinational, or global?
  o Learn about the company's values and organizational culture by reading about them in the Web site or in trade and business magazines.
  o Then, armed with information about the company, ask some broad, overarching blue sky questions.

- Two: "Can you describe to me: the division, group, subsidiary, facility that I'll be working in?"

  o At this point, you may ask about the team or division that you might be working in—its mission, its location, its operating principles.
  o Try to determine the degree of autonomy of this group or division from the parent or corporate entity.

- Three: "Can you give me some insight about the team, hiring manager, peers that I'll be working with?"

  o Now that you have carefully and logically approached the subject, you can ask questions about the person you'll be reporting to (you may not yet know them, if you are on your first telephone or personal interview).

o   You can ask about your peers, their styles of work, and their day to day practices.

Why is it important to ask the above questions in the order suggested? Because human nature being what it is, if you start in the opposite order, you'll soon digress into smaller and smaller details and never have the opportunity to ask questions in levels 1 and 2. By asking questions in this order, it also shows that you are interested in the whole entity and your potential effectiveness within it, not just in your parochial personal job concerns.

Preparing for the Second Interview

How do you stand out like mad during your second interview?
How do I differentiate myself from other more experienced
candidates? Do I bring a pizza or ride in on a unicycle?
—Alison Martínez, from one of her e-mails

It depends on the signals they gave you on the first interview.

What problems did they say need to be addressed? To the extent that you picked up on the problems that they are currently experiencing, you need to demonstrate that you can address them with your skills, knowledge, and attributes. This way you're ahead of the person who was not paying attention.

All employers have problems that need solving, or they have plans that they want to deploy. Even if the former incumbent was very good in his or her job, there are always ways to improve the situation. The point is—identify the problem (if you're not sure what it is, just ask! *You will get points for wanting to know.)* Then propose a solution, or at least a vision of how to make improvements, ways to make things better. Make sure you ask all the pertinent questions about this—to send a signal that you are interested in their problems, their agendas, and their future.

Second and third interviews are often very much like the first but with different people. They can be quite boring to an experienced candidate with a history of many interviews. Use the same process, that is, begin asking at the highest level, continuing through the division level down through.

Tips and Tactics for Interviewing

It goes without saying that you have to research the company with whom you are interviewing. So why do I go on and state the obvious? Because some people fail to do it. The Internet has made researching any company, or any topic, very easy. No need to look for news items about your target company through dusty periodicals in the public library. It's easy to research your target company; it leaves you no excuse for not having done it.

Make sure you understand the history of the company. This is particularly true for companies founded by individuals who have achieved iconic status like Microsoft (Bill Gates), Apple (Steve Jobs), Dell (Michael Dell), FedEx (Freddie Smith).

This notion also holds true in regional markets. If you live in a community like Rochester, New York, it would be inexcusable if you applied for a position at Paychex and had not heard of its founder (Tom Golisano) or at Constellation Brands (Robert and Richard Sands) or Wegmans Supermarkets (Robert Wegman, now deceased) or PAETEC (Arunas Chesonis).

Do's and Don'ts for Interviewing

Do: dress appropriately for the interview. This is where inside information is very helpful. Some companies allow wide amplitude in business wear and rarely insist on white shirt and ties. But others stick to what they think will work best with their clients. One very successful company in Rochester is noted for its dress code—and conduct—including entry doors reserved for the customers and visitors, another one for managers, and another one for the balance of employees.

Don't: sit in front of the person interviewing you in a perfectly symmetrical position. If you are sitting in a chair with arms, lean slightly to one side or the other. In other words, the left side of your body should look different than the right side. Why is this important? It denotes that you're comfortable, confident, and able to handle this situation without being overly stiff or rigid.

One time my employer sent me to California to investigate a race discrimination case. One of the persons that I had to interview was a vice president of the division. She was a minority female, and when she came to meet with me, she was clearly apprehensive and skeptical. She didn't like having to participate in this sort of thing. I sensed that, and I knew I had to defuse the situation to obtain her cooperation. As we sat down, the lady sat across the table from me, symmetrically, with her hands folded in front of her on top of the table. She appeared tense. I adopted a very relaxed sitting posture. Leaning back in the arm chair, I crossed my left leg over my right and used a note pad on my lap to write down her responses. My tone of voice was relaxed, my demeanor conveyed that I had done this many times, and I knew what had to be done, efficiently. After some dialogue over several minutes, I saw that she also leaned back on her chair, eventually crossed one leg over the other, and started swinging her high heel shoe from the tip of her toes. I knew then that she was onboard. She cooperated in her role, and the investigation was successfully concluded.

Do: be punctual. If you've never been to the location of the interview, give yourself extra time: what if there is an accident on the expressway? What if you can't find the building in a large industrial complex?

Don't: fly in on the morning of the interview—so many things can go awry. For interviews that require long distance travel, arriving the night before greatly improves the chances of being on time. Many airlines are booked solid, and sometimes flights are canceled due to lack of airplanes.

Do: give a firm handshake. Look the person in the eye as you shake hands. If necessary, repeat their name to make sure you have it. It will help you get it right and remember it. Better to repeat it now, during introductions, rather than forget what it was and be embarrassed later.

Don't: volunteer negative information. Be truthful about the question being asked, but don't add negative content that wasn't asked for. For example, if the hiring manager asks, "Why did you leave that job?" You can tell her, "Because they wanted someone with more marketing experience, and I decided I'd rather concentrate on web services." You should not say, "Because my manager was a self-centered, controlling, detail-obsessed, micromanager with delusions of grandeur, who would not even consider any other opinion."

Do: be polite and very courteous to the clerical or support staff that you meet at the interview location. That should go without saying, but it's often overlooked, and it can be part of the deciding factors. Here is an example of what can be done. As I was drafting this book, I had occasion to interview in a Fortune 500 company. There were six interviews scheduled for that day; and one person, a recruiting coordinator named Idris, had made all the arrangements, which I know is a lot of painstaking detailed work. After the interviews, I sent the customary personalized thank-you letters to each of my interviewers. But I also sent one to Idris even though I had not met her. She replied within minutes by e-mail—she was so excited to receive her own thank-you letter! It's obvious this had not happened to her before.

This reminds me of another story. When I was in high school, I attended a party at a beautiful apartment in New York City. After being there for a while, I went downstairs, outside, to get some fresh air. I then struck up a conversation with an older fellow, also standing outside. He said he worked in the TV and movie industry as a grip. I remarked that it must be exciting to meet and work among television and movie stars. He said, "Yes, it is," and that he always told them one thing: "Be nice to me on your way up because I'm still going to be here on your way down." I have never forgotten that advice.

Don't: look away or down at your feet when your host is talking to you. Look them in the eye and respond with nods or shaking of the head as appropriate to let her/him know you've understood.

Do: listen to the entire question before answering it. This becomes particularly hard as you become a more experienced candidate and after many interviews. It's important to discipline yourself to wait until the entire question has been asked.

Don't: chew gum or candy or fidget or ramble or slouch (see above for body language).

Do: allow the hiring managers to do most of the talking, if they are so inclined. Many hiring managers will spend forty-five out of sixty minutes describing the job, the company, the management, the joys of golf in Pebble Beach, whatever. Then, at the end they'll say, "I've had the most enjoyable interview with you!" Take it in stride. That person will go and tell all the others what a wonderful (listener) candidate you are. It's true.

Don't: discuss your salary expectations too early in the game. If you've done your homework, particularly with insiders, you should know that they will offer you something within 10 to 15 percent of your targeted salary. If your expectations are exceedingly high or if their pay practices are below the norm, you were not meant for each other.

Do: ask open questions that require the interviewer to reveal information. One tip given to me by a sales professional is that if the interviewer is not very cooperative, or seems to be holding back, you can say, "Oh?" in a voice tone as in, "Really?" or "Is that a fact?" It compels the interviewer to explain more.

Don't: ask closed questions that can be easily answered with a yes or a no.
Do: smile.

Papi, in the last half hour or so I did an internet search on second interviews and looked at about 10 websites. They don't even come close to the depth you have here in your book!
Alison Martínez, from one of her e-mails

My daughter, Alison, had been following my suggestion—always, always keep looking. She was a finalist for three fund raising positions in the Rochester, New York, area. One hiring manager went as far as saying to her in her last interview, "You're definitely what we're looking for. Just let me discuss it with my manager. When can you start?" But within two days, she received three letters and phone calls informing her that she was not the chosen candidate. Just like that. She went from almost celebrating a new position that she was assured was hers to nothing. You can imagine how upset she was.

My wife and I sat down with Alison and listened to her description of the kinds of jobs she had interviewed for, the environments that she would have been working in, and the attributes of the people that she had met. It became apparent that there were gaps, sometimes even polar differences, in their attributes and how they each viewed the world, which may have made her tenure in any of these positions disagreeable or impossible. Now, that may sound like a sour grapes story, but there is also another side, that as one door (or three doors) closes, other doors open. Alison kept on looking and applying for positions even as she knew she was a finalist. Within a few days, she was called back to interviews for a fund raising position at her alma mater, the University of Rochester, to meet with the dean of academic affairs, the chief administrative officer, and the president of the university hospital. Incredible. Even I, the skeptic, began to believe that she was finally close to landing. But it was not to be. She received more rejection letters—from her alma mater!

Handling Rejection

Job search is 100 percent rejection, because as soon as you land a job,
the search is over.
—Orville Pierson

It was, I must admit, a difficult time for her and for us. She had been unemployed for five months since coming back from the Galapagos Islands, where she had been a volunteer—teaching English. It was tough to keep up her spirits in spite of so many close calls without job offers. Her savings were dwindling, and she was depressed about the way she was treated by coworkers at a local coffee shop. The way Alison faced into it was by sticking with her overall strategy—keep looking, keep networking, following up on every lead.

d at a prominent not-for-profit organization. She and annual giving manager, a sizeable title and ilities for a young person. She attributes her success f, putting her attributes up front, and doing all the

GETTING THERE
Your Guide to the Summit

Luis A. Martínez, SPHR / CCP

PO Box 242
Pittsford, NY 14534
585. 766. 9536

Luis@HumanCapitalSP.com
www.gettingtherecoach.com

PO Box 242
Pittsford, NY 14534
585. 766. 9536

Luis@HumanCapitalSP.com
www.gettingtherecoach.com

Handle Exploratory Interviews

view is simply a conversation that you request with npany. This form of interviewing is a tool that you

company,
ewing skills,
ork,
s,
g managers that you are in a search, and
to work in that organization.

s that are raised during an exploratory interview itioned above. The only difference is that in an are not discussing a particular vacancy in the organization. Instead you are sensing your way around with your questions, trying to see what problems they have in their organization, and how your skills, experience, and attributes may be brought to bear on them. Likewise, the person(s) interviewing you are sensing how you may be able to help them.

Notice that I said that an exploratory interview is a conversation. That's how it should feel. It is not a presentation. It is not a lecture or a monologue of your skills and experience. It's more akin to meeting someone at your favorite watering hole and discussing your career with them. It should feel light, interesting, and even fun. It's critical that they see you as you are. If they don't like how you really are, you don't belong there, and this is the best way to find out.

The Purpose of This Interview Is—
To Get the Next Interview!

During your preparation for and throughout your interview process, you must bear in mind your key objective, which is to be such a compelling candidate that they'll just have to call you back for the next round of interviews. To hope or believe that your first interview will result in a job offer is incompatible with all but the most inconsequential of jobs. If you are applying at the Dairy Queen, the franchise owner may offer you a position as a cashier at the end of the first interview. But if you want to manage opening and closing the store along with the second or third shift of DQ employees, she will probably want to think about it, check your references, and ask you back (you hope) for a second round.

What Are They Really Buying? Your Attributes!

This is particularly true in higher levels of operations management, strategy, or planning positions. An engineer may become a vice president of strategy; a CPA/MBA become a chief technology officer; a PhD in physical chemistry becomes a worldwide vice president general manager; a master's level electrical engineer becomes chief operating officer (those are just a few real examples). I have known these men and women personally, and the reason they were chosen for those positions was one word—their *attributes*.

It's Really about Turning Your Passion into Opportunity

Throughout the interview process, it's essential that your passion and love for what you do come through. If you can't get jazzed up about the position for which you are interviewing, then there may be one of two problems: the position is not what you love to do, or you haven't been true to yourself when writing about what you love to do!

As the interview progresses, if it's right for you, it should become evident in your demeanor, your tone of voice, etc.

This is not the time to be shy and coy. Your body language should exude desire and appetite for the opportunity. It should be obvious to anyone that you are very enthusiastic for the position in question (but not desperate—desperation is a different energy).

When done properly, you are, in fact, turning your passion into cash.

A Good Interviewer Is Hard to Find

It is quite conceivable that as you go through a number of interviews in several companies, you will become quite adept at being interviewed and responding. There is a sweet taste of success in that, I think, because many managers are not talented interviewers.

Some hiring managers conduct interviews only once every few years, or they are totally wrapped up in their daily routine and have not adequately prepared to see you. In such circumstances, your challenge becomes keeping your patience while they squirm and struggle before you! Mind you, this doesn't mean that you are a shoe-in for the job—the fact that you are a superb interviewee does not ipso facto result in a job offer. In fact, if you don't handle yourself properly and with humility, an unprepared or insecure interviewer may hold it against you that you are "so smart."

Always bring extra copies of your resume to the interview. Some managers have totally forgotten that they have an appointment with you and can't get their hands on your resume, which they saw in their PC a few weeks before.

In general, utilize concrete examples and accomplishments. Keep your answers brief and to the point, your responses to questions positive. Ask your questions as suggested above. Thank the interviewer.

Then, as any sales professional will tell you, "Ask for the order," e.g., ask for the next interview. Say something like this: "Now that you've seen how my skills and experience can help you with your business issues, when can I expect to come back and meet other members of the organization?"

Make sure you understand the next steps.

Smile.

How to Handle the Telephone Interview

When you investigate a position it may result in a telephone interview situation. Many times the phone interview comes as a surprise. It pays to do your homework and find out if candidates are going to be screened by telephone. If you find out that such is the case, then there are some things you can do to prepare.

- Keep your resume and information about that company close by your phone, so you can instantly refer to it when on the phone.
- The anonymity of a phone interview may seduce you into overfamiliarity. Remain formal and appropriately deferential through the conversation. Everything counts. There is no such thing as "off the record." If you don't want someone to hear about it, don't say it.
- Allow the interviewer to do most of the talking, if that's their inclination.
- Expand your answers positively beyond "yes" or "no."
- Speak directly into the phone, enunciating clearly and distinctly. Chances are the interviewer is writing furiously, taking notes.
- Take your own notes.
- Ask for an on-site interview, for example: "I really appreciate that you took the time to evaluate my credentials for this position. Will you be calling me back to come out to your facility and meet other members of your organization?"
- Smile. Yes, even on the phone, they will "see" your smile.

This actually happened to me as I was drafting this book. I was finishing up a networking meeting with a colleague at a local coffee shop. As we were getting up to leave, my cell phone rang. The caller identified herself as Ann Maynard, the recruiter from an important Fortune 500 company. I had just applied to that company online only hours before! Ann said, "Can I ask you a few questions?" So I said, "Sure!" thinking that she wanted to set up a date and time for a telephone interview. But as the conversation progressed, it became obvious to me that *she was interviewing me right then and there.* What's worse, about ten minutes into the interview, the coffee shop manager informed me that the shop was closed and was asking me to leave. Covering the mouthpiece on my cell phone, I put on this look of grave concern and pleaded with the shop manager, "Please, it's a job interview, please let me finish, just a few more minutes?" He reluctantly agreed, and I continued my conversation with Ann.

Fortunately, I had done my homework about that company *before* I actually applied online, so that in fact she did not catch me unprepared. I had even researched what they were willing to pay for that position, and when Ann asked me my salary expectations, I was ready with my response, and it was within their parameters.

My telephone interview with Ann was successful, and it was followed with a lunch meeting with Ann, plus six other interviews in person at the company. So the point is you should do your homework and prepare for the telephone interview even before you apply online.

Immediately After the Interview

As soon as you leave the office or building where you had your interview, it's critical that you evaluate the process you just underwent. Take down some notes:

- Whom did you meet? Names and titles.
- What did each of them say?
- What did they ask, and why would they have asked that? This points to where the problems are which with your skills, experience, and attributes you hope you can solve.
- What aspects of the interview went well? Poorly?
- What was said during the last few minutes of the interview? Was the interviewer really glad to meet you? Did s/he hint or say they'll recommend you for next level of interviewing? *This holds the key to whether you will be called back.*
- Always send a thank-you letter. This can be done as an e-mail, but it's a formal e-mail complete with your identifying contact information and signed (electronically). Read the section below, "The New World of E-Mail."
- After a few days, call to follow up. Again, express your gratitude for the opportunity to interview.

On Exchanging Business Cards

One of the important rituals of the exploratory interview, and certainly of all networking practices, is the exchange of business cards.

Now, why would I devote an entire section to this? Well, because,

- it's important, and
- many people fail to do it.

Exchanging business cards is important because, when done properly, it breaks the ice in the early part of the conversation, helps both you and your host or hostess to relax, and it can be used to generate questions or comments which are more focused and have greater value than just bantering about the weather. How so? Well, let's take the exchange of business cards step by step, and you'll see how this simple but effective ritual can add value to your job search.

If you're looking for free business cards, try this: *http://www.vistaprint.com*

They provide good quality cards, inexpensively, but make sure you pay the twenty bucks to take the vistaprint advertisement off the back of the card!

For Exploratory Interviews

When you visit an organization for an exploratory interview, you will typically be introduced by administrative staff to your host or hostess, and then typically you proceed to shake hands and greet them. Be prepared by proceeding as follows:

- After they ask you to sit down, you should reach into your portfolio or briefcase (and I mean *brief* case) and take out one of your business cards.
- You can then say, "May I give you my business card? It has my contact information."
- Then, after your host accepts it, you can say, "And do you have a business card?"
- If your host hands you a business card, pause for a moment and *read it!* This is an opportunity for you to ask one or two questions about its contents and immediately launch into a conversation.
- The worst thing you can do is to accept your host's business card and stick it in your pocket without bothering to look at it. That's a lost opportunity to start the conversation, and in Asian cultures, that's considered very rude behavior—a diss.

For Networking Meetings

- Before you go to a networking meeting, make sure you have about a dozen of your business cards in your pocket. What I do is put my business cards in my shirt pocket (*nothing* else in there, you don't want a pocket protector full of multicolored pens).
- As you introduce yourself to someone, reach into your shirt pocket and offer them your business card.
- Then ask them for their business card. If they give you one, you must stop, look at it, and read it. Ask them one or two questions about

it. As noted above, in Asian cultures this is a refined art. What you should take away from that is that a business card is an extension of the professional entity of the person, to be treated with due respect.

- After a brief exchange of information, put their card in your briefcase or in a special place in your purse (not in the back pocket of your pants and not in your shirt pocket because it will be mixed up with your own cards).
- Ladies will have to be more creative about where to keep their own cards, maybe in a side pouch of their purse or briefcase or in the right pocket of their suit jacket. Ladies should not be fumbling through all the contents of their purse, as I've often witnessed, to get down to a card holder. (One evening, at a networking meeting I offered my business card to a lady and she accepted it; then I asked her for her business card, and she actually asked me to hold out my two hands as she emptied the many contents of her large purse into my outstretched hands until she found a little card case at the very bottom. We just laughed . . .)
- The motion to retrieve and offer your own business card should be smooth and practiced.

As soon as you get home or back to your office, take their business cards and write a few notes on the back, such as the date and venue of the event, their sports or hobbies, maybe their alma mater; whatever you can remember that will help you later in another conversation with them.

By the way, these business cards you collect are not just for you. They are to be shared with others who from time to time need your help. You should see these cards as a vehicle for helping to connect people. When someone calls you with questions about other people or enterprises, you should be able to refer to your box or folder of business cards and give them two or three names and numbers. Remember, you would want someone to do the same for you.

There are software tools that can help you organize your contact list. ACT! is one of the popular contact and customer manager tools that helps you organize contact information, manage daily responsibilities, and communicate with your network contacts to improve your productivity. Tools like ACT! have many individual and corporate customers, and they are an effective solution for anyone who regularly works with contacts.

The ritual of exchanging business cards is not very complicated. But I'm appalled at the number of people who, during networking meetings and interviews, actually tell me that they don't own any business cards or didn't bring any. I make it clear to my clients that I expect them to go into interviews and networking meetings armed with business cards, and that they engage in the ritual of exchange as suggested above.

What about Working with Headhunters?

Many ask me what to do about executive recruiters. Should they approach recruiters? What's the likelihood that a recruiter will help them land a job? How good is the reputation of recruiters?

As with any other endeavor, there are mostly good recruiters, but there are a few that can leave one with a bad taste. The main concept to keep in mind when dealing with recruiters is that they don't work for you. They work for the hiring manager who is paying them a fee to find and screen candidates.

This means that when you write to a search consultant or contingency fee recruiter, they're not going to be of much help to you unless they happen to have a search assignment that coincidently happens to require someone with your knowledge, skills, and attributes. If that's the case, you are fortunate, and now you've got their attention.

Among your many activities in your job search you'll have to decide how much time to spend on writing to and meeting with recruiters. There are thousands across the land and there hundreds even in a medium-size city. While it's not a complete waste of time to send a cover letter and resume to a search consultant, you have to work it into your overall priority matrix. If you think, however, that by corresponding with a few of them, even the very prestigious ones, all you have to do now is sit back and wait for the phone to ring, you'll be wasting your time.

Working with search consultants is not your first priority. *Networking is your first priority.* Your networking list should include some of the prominent search consultants in your region. If you are already doing a good job of networking and now want to work more closely with recruiters, here is a way to work with them.

If you are going to approach a *contingency search* recruiter, keep in mind that they don't get paid by the hiring company until and unless you are hired. That's why they are called contingency recruiters—because they only get paid contingent on the hiring manager actually hiring a candidate presented by the contingency recruiter. You have to be careful with contingency recruiters. The way they work is like this: if you send them your cover letter and resume and they happen to like it because they think your skills are marketable, they will simply mask your personal identifying information with their recruiter contact information and attach your resume to an e-mail blast to every company they know, in hopes one of them will be interested in your skills and experience. Your entire resume will be visible to hundreds, except for your name and address, and it may actually end up in the hands of your current company's human resource director.

A *retained search* firm behaves differently. They are retained by the company which has a vacancy, and the recruiter gets paid his or her fee even if the search does not turn up a suitable candidate. The fee is typically 33 percent of the first year cash compensation of the newly hired employee. The downside of working with retained search firms is that you would have to write to a great many of them, in the hopes that one has been retained to look for someone like you.

By the way, even when a retained search firm calls you, you should be very well prepared. I received a call one time from a female search consultant in a firm based in California. She had heard of me through someone else (networking is always my first priority), and she thought I might be interested in a position as a vice president of human resources for a well-known eye care pharmaceutical company. The headhunter had left me a phone message with enough hints that I readily figured out the client company she was representing. I went through the Internet and researched the company and garnered a lot of information about their governance, complete with the names of the top leaders and with the name of the person I would be reporting to.

When the search consultant finally caught up with me live on the phone, I began asking her a number of questions using information from the research I had just completed. To my utter surprise, I was way ahead of her about information concerning the reporting relationships, dynamics of the different corporate entities, and implications for the position for which I would be interviewing. The gist of it was that I turned down the opportunity because she did not know that the position in question reported to a vice president of international human resources, who in turn reported to the corporate vice president of human resources, so the position in question was something I would have aspired to about twenty years ago. I even knew the names of the vice presidents and had their bios (which were readily available on their company's Web site), information which I used to quickly educate the recruiter.

If she wasn't embarrassed by this, she had no professional shame. Why my adamant tone? She had been paid a princely sum to conduct a search for an executive and had failed to do even the most rudimentary research about the company's senior management team and was oblivious to information about the persons to whom the vacant position would report. All this information was available publicly on the Internet.

The New World of E-mail

Electronic mail has virtually totally replaced hard copy as the medium for communication among employers and job candidates. The perceived anonymity and informality of the e-mail medium can lead one astray. It's important to keep some principles in mind:

- With the first message to a target employer, or even to a networking contact, you should establish a sense of respect and formality. For example, don't begin your e-mail to a hiring manager by saying "Hi," Address her/him formally, as Dear Mr. or Dear Ms., or even Dear Dr.
- Your cover letter can be included in the body of the e-mail, although preferably as an attachment in standard, updated software like Microsoft Word. But be cognizant that increasingly, some hiring managers may be using personal computing devices, like the Blackberry device, which may not be able to open attachments.
- Your resume can likewise be an attachment in MS Word, although you have to check to make sure that the recipient is able to open the attachment.
- Make sure you don't have cute or religious or pontificating sign-offs at the bottom of your e-mail. No one is amused by your attempt at humor or at proselytizing for politics or religion or even for dietary supplements.

Chapter Summary

The content of this chapter suggests that there are three tools in preparation for the interview. With the first tool, you learned about the first question that you will be asked by the interviewer, which is "Tell me about yourself" or one of its many variants. This question should always elicit from you your elevator speech, but the elevator speech should be adjusted and adapted to the context of the question and circumstances.

This chapter also discussed the purpose of behavioral interview questions, which types you are likely to experience, and how to turn them into a potent portrait of your skills, knowledge, and attributes. It also points out questions that may arise which may feel awkward to you, and some may even be illegal. Suggestions for overcoming them were presented.

Emphasis was made about preparation for interviews using the T-chart for interviewing, which is the best tool to use for practiced preparation. Preparation also means that you need to analyze and be cognizant of the needs of the employer. Tips were suggested on educating the potential employer about your contributions and potential value to them.

There are a number of questions that you must ask your interviewer followed by tips and tactics for successful interviewing. A long list of Do's and Don'ts for interviewing was also presented. The reality of rejection and how to handle it was discussed. There was a section concerning how to handle exploratory interviews. The chapter emphasized that the purpose of the first interview is to get the second interview, the purpose of the second is to get the third, and so on.

The section posed the question: What are they really buying? Your attributes! It suggests that it's really about turning your passion into opportunity. After you have interviewed for several opportunities in different companies, you will be very experienced and most likely realize that a good interviewer is hard to find.

You have to be ready to handle the telephone interview, and this chapter has provided some tips and tactics. What to do immediately after the interview is an important topic. Exchanging business cards is an important part of networking, and there is a discussion on how to do it during an exploratory interview or during networking meetings. If you want to work with search consultants, you should understand how the advantages and disadvantages. The new world of e-mail presents some challenges that many of the readers had never anticipated. Finally, we move to the homework section.

Homework

1. Gather all information and data points from all sources—job postings, telephone interviews, informants inside the company, people connected in some way to the targeted company, Web site information, web browser information, etc.
2. Using attachment D, the T-Chart for interviewing, make a list of what you think are the target company's business problems, their needs or issues on the left side of the T-Chart, in order of priority based on your understanding.

3. On the right side of the T-Chart, write down your skills and experience that you can quote to the interviewer as potential solutions to their business problems.
4. If you don't have skills or experience that you can directly apply to one or more of their problems, then list one or more of your attributes that would enable you to solve their problem.
5. Do this homework and rehearse your answers out loud. This is key, it's very important that you not only do the intellectual research and write the answers, but that you also *rehearse these answers*. Why? To build neuropathways, which will let you respond quickly and accurately to their questions. This is what athletes do to prepare for important competitive events.
6. Make up a sunshine folder for yourself.

Friday, May 25, 2007

You changed my life! You made me put me first, and no one has ever made me put me first. No one ever asked me "And what do you want for yourself?" I'm getting rid of all the people who were hanging on me, feeding off of me, sucking me dry. But you, Luis—you get to stay in my inner circle.

—Rachelle Evans, after she dumped a horrible employer, followed every step of this job search process, and landed a payroll manager position in Phoenix, Arizona, her desired destination.

FOUR

CAREER COACHING 104—
The Compensation Discussion

One question I am often asked is, what's the best time in the job search process to discuss salary?

That's a lot like when people ask me, "What's a good car to buy?" Well, the answer to either of these depends on many factors. The question about salary negotiation is difficult to answer because it depends on many aspects of the yet-fragile relationship between you as the candidate and your potential employer. I think it's counterproductive to say, "Always do this" or "Always do that." My suggestion is simply that *you should be prepared and be flexible* about when and how to discuss salary.

The best preparation for the salary negotiation begins with research of the market pay rate for your desired position *prior* to approaching the employer—even before you draft the cover letter. Once you send your cover letter and resume by e-mail, you might receive a response within hours inviting you to a quick telephone screen where they may suddenly ask you, "And what are your salary expectations?" If you haven't already done your homework, you'll be caught flat-footed and perhaps ruin your chances for a good starting salary or conversely ruin your chances for a second interview (read my story about this very circumstance in chapter 3, How to Handle the Telephone Interview).

So for starters, make sure that you know the worth of your desired position. Go to the Web and do an Internet search; query various sources and arrive at a minimum, a midpoint, and a maximum for your desired position. Be cognizant that the value of the position can be very different depending on geography. An accountant position in Hot Springs, Arkansas, pays differently than in New York City or San Francisco.

Do some research about salary information in the Internet for your desired position; then do some simple arithmetic to arrive at the average salary being paid. One good rule of thumb is to throw out the highest and lowest numbers you find. For example, if your are researching salaries for a mechanical engineering position with five years of experience and you find the lowest salary is $28,000 and the highest is $71,000, throw out those two as they are too far apart and are likely skewed by some undetermined factor.

What if They Ask My Salary?

In my view, it doesn't matter to me if the employer wants to know your salary *expectations* during the first interview as long as

a. you have had a chance to tell them all that you are worth, in terms of skills, knowledge, and attributes;
b. you have done your homework so you have an informed guess about their pay practices and;
c. you provide them only your salary *expectations,* not your current salary nor your W-2 information.
d. If they insist on knowing your current salary, simply reply that this information will be forthcoming as the interview process develops further, and if you are still interested in pursuing the opportunity (and thus your negotiation process has begun).

It is reasonable for an employer to require two previous years of W-2 information when they are trying to verify information you provided *about sales commissions earned or performance bonuses received or stock options granted.* But you should make this available to verify your salary expectations only when it's clear that you are the *finalist,* and that they have an offer pending for you contingent on verification of your income.

Remember, you are entering this first interview having done your homework, so now you have a very educated guess about what the position should pay. Here's what you should do to get ready for this first interview:

a. Use your network to penetrate the employer (find someone who works there) and understand the kind of compensation schemes they have, e.g., are they well organized with rigorous job classifications and compensation ranges? Or are they a family-owned enterprise where the big boss makes all salary decisions using her best hunch?

b. Do your Internet homework and make sure you understand the min/mid/max for this position, give or take $1,000 per annum.

c. Know your own numbers, that is, know the minimum that you will accept and the most desirable but reasonable salary you will achieve for this particular position in this geographical area.

Negotiating for the Optimal Salary

Total compensation can take many forms, and the higher the position within the organization, the more creatively one can approach this important topic.

Here's what not to do. One of my clients was in the process of negotiating his starting salary and total compensation package. He was a finalist for the chief financial officer position at a regional not-for-profit. He became obsessed with a number that he wanted; it was around $104,000. And after much to and fro, he lost the opportunity because of his single-minded pursuit of that figure.

Fundamentally his approach failed because he did not take into account the many forms that compensation can take. Base starting salary is just one form. For a position like his, there was opportunity to negotiate for a sign-on bonus, a better office, country club dues, professional conference fees, guaranteed bonus after six months/twelve months/eighteen months, clerical support, company car, accelerated salary review, larger budget, larger staff, attendance at exclusive senior management or board of directors meetings, performance-based increments, etc. The list is as long as his imagination. But he was obsessed with a specific number, and they gave the job to someone else. He ended up doing financial audits with out-of-state clients, traveling frequently away from his family, which he really didn't want.

So after all this work you've done to get to this point, don't blow it now with an adversarial encounter with your new employer. The process of negotiating starting salary and other benefits commensurate with the position is collaborative, not adversarial. You must see this simply as a problem-solving process, wherein you get on the "same side of the table" with your new manager and try to resolve the issue. This takes creativity and great interpersonal skills—consider it your first work assignment!

Here's another way to view it—you are helping your new boss solve a compensation issue. Be creative and resourceful. Be pleasant and cooperative. Help her/him see that you believe this to be a problem to be solved by *both* of you, so don't just hand over the issue of your compensation and walk away as if it's totally her problem.

If you find yourself on the opposite side of the table, with an increasingly bellicose discussion, ask for a day or two to think things over, a strategic retreat to let tempers cool. Ask yourself, where is the common ground? Have you reached accord on any aspects of the job or remuneration? If you want more than they are willing to give, can you do more, that is, can you accept other responsibilities so they see your value added in exchange for the compensation you want?

The main idea is to recognize the box s/he is in and to facilitate and problem solve toward what you want.

What if You Can't Come to Terms?

Let's face it, you don't have much leverage, particularly if you're unemployed and have no other offers in hand. This is why it's so important to always keep looking so that you can obtain two or more offers and have some leverage at the salary negotiating table.

If you are stuck, mired in arguments, you have to decide among all the competing positives and negatives of the offer and conclude to either work with it or keep looking.

On a positive note for you, it's not a good idea for a company to continually hammer down starting salaries. People hired under such salary practices soon become savvy that there are better paying opportunities and leave for better terms. Turnover of this sort is a costly problem for an enterprise.

Think broadly. Some things to take into consideration, for example, are opportunities for advancement. While I was in the US government, I was approached by the regional director and asked if I would be interested in switching career tracks from community relations to program management. The move required me to take a step back in grade and pay. I took a pay cut of 17 percent and began work as a supervisor in training. In that career change, I learned all about supervision; and in less than two years, I had been promoted twice and passed my original salary. More importantly, I was on my way to a rewarding career with much higher pay in management.

Chapter Summary

In this section you learned the main point, which is that the compensation discussion should not be an adversarial encounter. In fact, you should see yourself on the same side of the table as your hiring manager; and in circumstances of significant pay and perks, you should definitely help your hiring manager with creative thoughts and ideas to make it work for you. The worst thing you can do is to have the attitude that "It's her problem, let her figure out how to pay me what I'm worth." Treat it instead as your very first administrative challenge in your new company.

If you encounter a roadblock, think about a strategic retreat. Oftentimes things have a way of working themselves out after a respite.

FIVE

CAREER COACHING 105—
The First One Hundred Days

Now that you've landed, what's the first thing you do?

This is a very uncomfortable space—the first few days. After you've found your way to the restroom, you need to put together a tactical plan and a strategic plan. Actually, you have to do both simultaneously as the tactical plan has to blend with and be a precursor and predictor of your strategic direction.

One of my clients used this book and, after some months of search, landed a job in a family-owned machine shop. She called me from time to time, and we had coffee so she could tell me how she was coming along. When I told her I was ready to write this section of the book, "The First One Hundred Days," she said, "I'll write it for you!"

I smiled when I read Cheri's e-mail, the content was so fresh, unvarnished, to the point. I just cut and pasted it. Here it is—Cheri Magin's ten recommendations for the first one hundred days on the job. I didn't change a word of what she said.

1. **Become a sponge!** There is so much to learn and it really does take longer than anyone wants it to. Take every opportunity to learn as much as you can from anyone and everyone. Say less, listen more.
2. **Be a good listener.** Really listen to what coworkers, peers and management are saying. Listen for the "unspoken" messages. Watch body language. Listen but do not give opinion or affirmation (especially to negativism). The more you listen the more people will tell you. This will help you learn the culture.

3. **Prove yourself.** All the achievements in the world will not matter when you walk into a new job. No one knows you and no one cares what you did in the past. Until you show what you can achieve you could be viewed suspiciously or as a threat. It is critical to show you can make a contribution and get along with people.

4. **Be a team player.** A team player may not only be in the conference rooms and on projects but also in less formal settings. Many work locations have lunch routines or breakfast clubs, after work social time or sports events. It may not be your thing, but to join in will help get to know the people and learn the politics of the workplace (and be accepted by peers).

5. **Adapt to the culture** if it is acceptable to you or find another job. Each workplace has a different culture. My 3 recent experiences were the corporate culture of a big company, a high end specialty retail store with a younger workforce, and now a predominately male machine shop culture! These 3 could not be more different. Learning to adapt is key.

6. **Be proactive** to ask for performance expectations and feedback. I scheduled a meeting after 30 days with my boss to discuss "how I was doing". I brought to the meeting a list of training accomplishments, training still needed, results achieved and future goals (short and long term). The 1/2 hour meeting lasted over an hour and achieved the goal of assuring that the boss was satisfied in the short time on the job. A request was made to schedule another meeting in the future.

7. **Look for ways to improve the workplace.** In my first week on the job, there was a company meeting where the communications to employees was very poor. The next day people were complaining about the meeting. Along with that the way some important HR policies were being communicated through email to a workforce that ran machines and were not comfortable with email communications. I saw a need for improved communications, so I suggested an Employee Newsletter. The idea was accepted by management. I took on the project and became the editor of the 1st employee newsletter (for a very small company) soliciting input from Management. It was one way for me to prove my abilities and get to know the people.

8. **Don't ask or expect special treatment.** Try to not take time off for appointments, sickness or even vacation during the 1st 100 days. Unless an agreement was made at the time of being hired of a need to take time off in the near future, it is best not to miss any days, if possible.

9. **Be positive!** Negative coworkers can result in a challenging workplace. Find strategies to fight negativism, hang with positive people, take walks for a break, listen to music (if possible), and focus on your goals.

10. **Stay in the job hunting mindset.** Keep your resume updated, continue to network, stay in touch with people who have common interests, and be involved in activities/clubs/volunteerism. There are no guarantees that any job is forever. Being mentally prepared is half way to accepting the next job hunting opportunity. The other half are the strategies in this book.

Cheri and I will stay in touch and see how this all works out. I think that point number 10 is very realistic. She's suggesting not to become complacent in the new position. It's a world economy now which results in a very dynamic business environment. Now I'll add my own three recommendations to Cheri's list above:

- **Meet the people around you:** Set up one-on-one meetings with them. After the warm-up questions about the weather, the kids, etc., ask them what they think needs to be done to improve things in the workplace, things that are within your sphere of influence. In other words, ask them how you can help make things better, and especially how you can help make things better *for them!*

- **Get results—quickly!** When you arrive at your new job, you will probably be asked to decide on a number of issues that have languished since your predecessor vacated the position. Sort the issues into three piles: easy decisions, studied decisions, and world hunger problems. Make your easy decisions quickly, so they can see results coming from you. This will help your hiring manager a lot because she bet on you, so now it's up to you to make her look good! For decisions requiring more study, form a small team of people with process knowledge. Schedule the first meeting to workshop the problem. But problems that look like world hunger are probably just that. Be careful how you become involved in those; they won't be done in one hundred days.

- **Anticipate, anticipate, anticipate:** Look ahead, discuss issues with those around you, and let them see you are accessible and easy to work with. Then use the information to anticipate what's around the bend. Anticipation—making informed guesses as to what lies ahead—is a very powerful tactic. You will look like a genius.

- **Ask for a mentor:** In many companies, this is a general practice—to have mentors assigned to persons new to the organization. That relationship with an experienced incumbent helps the new employee get acclimated and become productive more quickly to mutual benefit.

Chapter Summary

Overall, it's important to set a good tone in the first one hundred days. Getting to know the people quickly and producing some tangible results are key. Listen more than talk, find some good quick hits to show some results. Leave the larger "world hunger" problems for another time.

Above all, find those people who are willing and able to help you, and listen to them.

SIX

TACTICAL SUPPORT

What would you do, if you weren't afraid?
—Spencer Johnson, MD, *Who Moved My Cheese?*

The Dangers of the Comfort Zone

Beleaguered and becalmed

Karen White* was working at her checkout register at Wegmans, the ubiquitous supermarket in upstate New York. Karen was in her early forties and was pleasant and conversational as she checked out my groceries on Wednesday nights. I had seen her from time to time, and while chatting with her, I learned that she liked jazz, so we often made small talk around that topic.

One evening, as I went to her register, I noticed that she was quite despondent; she didn't want to engage in the usual chatter.

Karen, are you okay?

Well, no, not really.

How can I help?

I'm having a very bad time. I'm holding this job and two other part-time jobs. My husband and I are not getting along and I have two girls in high school, and I just don't know what I'm going to do.

I learned that Karen was in the process of getting separated from her husband, and she was trying to keep it all together with paying bills and supporting her two daughters. Karen was very distraught.

> *Look, Karen, here's my card. I provide career coaching services. If you call me or send me an e-mail, we could get together for an hour, and maybe I can help you get a better paying job so you don't have to work three jobs, okay?*
>
> *Okay, I'll send you an e-mail.*

A few days later I received an e-mail. The sender was *Mom_slave@[emailserver].com*. I scratched my head. Was this a prank? Who would name herself Mom Slave? Implications about the sender's psyche came to mind—who is this that evidently feels so poorly about herself? Why would someone announce that she's a slave to her children or to others? In just a few seconds, a torrent of suppositions and conjecture flooded my mind.

I opened the e-mail, and the sender identified herself—Karen White.

Karen wanted to take me up on my offer for some career coaching, and we agreed to meet in a coffee shop.

I confess that it did not go as well as I had hoped. I interviewed her in my usual way, but her demeanor was such that she thought she didn't even deserve that anyone should try to help her. As I proceeded with my usual questions, it became evident that she had come to believe that she had no skills, and that she did not have much to offer. We took longer than usual to get some information down about what she loves to do, her skills, and her attributes. I remember she wrote very little about herself. Maybe it was situational, given her current state with the crisis in her family. But I suspect that it had been going on much longer; for example, her e-mail address, Mom Slave, had not been made up recently. I believe she had had this e-mail address for some time, evidence of a longer term condition.

Karen promised me she would do the homework for Career Coaching 101. Some weeks went by, and I had not heard from her. I looked her up at the Wegmans store, but they told me she had resigned. I lost track of Karen. But I think of her from time to time, and of many more like her who have met with me, spent one or two or more hours working with me, but to my knowledge didn't change anything. They haven't done anything different, so they can't move out of their familiar zone nor advance from their current state.

Was it my process that didn't work? Is it this book and its method that failed them?

I think not.

With all due respect to them, I think it was not the failure of the method or of the coaching process.

One observation I have made over the years is how people settle into a comfort zone and remain there in spite of predictable and often dire consequences.

Comfort zones take as many shapes and configurations as there are circumstances in life. Some people fail to educate themselves sufficiently and later in life have the consequences of poor-paying jobs or chronic unemployment. Others stay in very unpleasant or even counterproductive occupations with terrible managers or working conditions because they are afraid of change, afraid of what might be.

> *If you're going through hell—keep going!*
> —Winston Churchill

The example presented by the story of Karen White has many parallels. I'll cite two more.

Comfort Zone Disposition = Disastrous Consequences

Back in 2003, I started a car and boat repair business with two other partners. One partner, we'll call him Rodney, was the factory certified automotive and marine technician. In our partnership, he was the seasoned service manager responsible for running our ten-thousand-square-foot facility and supervising all other technical assistants. The third partner, Jason, was a professional sales representative with a great deal of automotive sales and service experience. Jason's responsibility was to be "on the street" selling to other smaller dealers and service shops to increase our business-to-business, as well as retail customer base.

My responsibility was to take care of all the administrative, banking, legal, regulatory, and personnel issues.

At first everything ran pretty well, and by early 2004, we had so much incoming business that we hired seven other people to handle the work flow. We noticed that Jason was spending a lot of time in the shop working on cars and giving mandates to all the other technicians, instead of putting feet on the street to drum up new business. Since we were doing fairly well, at this point it appeared academic to address it, so we didn't pursue it. But consequences were soon upon us.

Two things became apparent over time—our employees were turning over very quickly, and our customers weren't returning, even though we were literally gaining one new customer every day, seven days a week. After much review, Rodney and I realized that Jason was not doing any selling; in fact, he spent a lot of time mistreating the employees and mishandling the customers.

We sat down with Jason, explained our findings, and asked him to go out every day and sell. But he didn't want to. He kept coming into the shop every morning, working on cars until after lunch, and then doing a very poor job of looking for new business. No matter how much we emphasized the fact that winter was coming in 2004 and we needed him to build us a reserve of automotive and boat repair projects to get us through the long cold winter in Rochester, he wouldn't budge.

Finally, in November I sat down with Jason.

> *Jason, here we are again, having this same discussion. Your responsibility in this partnership is to sell, and you haven't brought in any new business in weeks.*

Jason said,

> *Well, I've been out there, believe me, and here's all the places and people I've been talking to.*

I could see he wasn't getting the point.

> *Yes, Jason, I see your handwritten list of names, but that does not constitute a prospect list. That's just the people you happen to know. Jason, you have to extend yourself to this whole market, which is four contiguous counties, especially in the profitable market for boat maintenance and repairs. We need to sign several large restoration projects to work on and carry us through this winter.*

Jason protested,

> *Look, I'm going out every day and trying.*

Exasperated, he left me no alternative.

Okay, Jason, here's the bottom line. We have been paying you out of operations. But the problem is that we have not had enough revenue from operations, and I have been writing personal checks to cover the difference. So effectively, I have been paying you out of my personal wallet. No more, Jason. This coming month, in December, you will be paid only from what we earn as gross margin from all the sales you personally make. So if you don't sell anything at a profit, we have no paycheck for you in December. Do you understand?

Jason understood. But astonishingly, he did not change one iota of his behavior.

In December 2004, he didn't sell anything, so we didn't pay him. He quit the business in January.

What point am I making? What lessons can we draw from these few examples? The main lesson that I've learned from observing the behaviors and experiences of some of my clients—and from the loss of my business—is that some people will continue to behave exactly as the day before, within their comfort zone, in spite of predictable and calamitous consequences for themselves and their dependent families. Jason had defined his comfort zone—he just wanted to come in and work on cars at his convenience; he wanted to boss the other employees around even though it was counterproductive, and he wasn't bringing in any new business. But Jason refused to change his behavior even though we had made the consequences eminently clear. He quit the business and went home—unemployed—and owing many thousands of dollars as a member of a failing business!

A Mole in His Hole

Here's one more example. One day one of my colleagues at work shared with me that her husband, Phillip,* with a doctorate in natural sciences, had been laid off nine months before:

Cherie, * *what was Phillip's position when he was laid off?*

He was teaching biology at the college.

So is he looking for another teaching position?

No, he's not looking at all! He goes to the basement every day and works with his woodworking tools making custom cabinets and furniture. Then when he sells that stuff to his customers, he barely gets what he paid for the wood, so he's making zero money and not looking for a job. I'm so frustrated with him!

Have you given him my business card? Have you told him that I can help him with career coaching?

Yes, yes, I've brought it up so many times, he gets mad at me. But he won't budge! He thinks that just e-mailing his resume once or twice a day is all he has to do. Meantime, I've had to go back to work to keep our healthcare benefits, and I'm supposed to be home raising my children!

Cherie, what are you going to do?

I'm going to take my two boys and leave him.

I was stunned. There were wedding photographs of Phillip and Cherie on her credenza in her office. I had known Cherie for several years, and here she is telling me that she's going to leave her husband of six years. I scrambled for an answer.

Cherie, we've been invited to a Christmas party next week, and I know you and Phillip were invited too. Do you mind if I approach Phillip at the party and see if I can persuade him to come to see me?

Go right ahead. I've done all I can. He is so hardheaded. I'm done with him. See what you can do.

At the party, I approached Phillip and emphasized to him that spending one hour with me going over my career-coaching method might make a difference. He agreed to meet me the following week at a coffee shop.

We met as agreed, and I conducted my usual interview using the tools in the first chapter. After some discussion about Career Coaching 101, I asked him to underline on his resume those things that appeared on his list of love to do. He tossed his resume back at me and said that there was nothing to underline.

Zero. Nada.

What Phillip had just done was to inform me that of all the things he had done, including his education to earn a PhD in science, of all those things—there were none he loved to do. He was the first client who ever said to me that he had never done anything he loved.

His resume was very busy but inscrutable. We started from scratch, which meant his resume had to be completely rebuilt. It took several days in January, but we got it done. He started sending his resume out, and in six weeks, he was working as a project manager for a new company, developing medical products.

Phillip did not know, at least not through me, how close he had come to losing his wife and family because of his wallowing in his comfort zone—puttering around the house and tinkering in his basement making cabinets. He had been unwilling to take the necessary steps to be in charge of his destiny, to create his own luck. But fortunately he turned a corner.

Today, more than a year later, I am happy to report that Phillip has been promoted to manager of a new product launched by the start-up company that he joined, which is making great strides.

And he saved his marriage.

Unemployed?

Opportunity is missed by most people because it is dressed in overalls and looks like work.
—Thomas A. Edison

Many a career has come apart on the shoals of layoffs, plant closures, budget cuts, failed mergers, and many other reasons. If you are one of those who is now unemployed, it is easy to fall into traps of self-pity, procrastination, recrimination, and other conscious or subconscious attempts to challenge reality. The good news is that there is an antidote to this paralysis.

The following is required behavior for the unemployed:

- Every day is a work day: shower, shave, put on your business clothes, and be at your work station from 8:00 a.m. to 5:00 p.m.

- Create in your home a work space that is solely dedicated to your job search—even if it's only a card table in the corner of your bedroom—when you go there, you are at work, not to be disturbed.
- If it's 2:00 p.m. and you're still in your bathrobe and slippers, you're in big trouble!
- Do the laundry and mow the lawn on nights and weekends.
- Make sure you have networking meetings on your calendar. You should have eight or ten each week.
- Try to arrange "coffee meetings" for networking in the mornings before work or even after work.
- Don't ask your network contact for lunch meetings as they require much more time and little gets done amid ordering and eating. Lunch meetings are more likely to be canceled because they take place in the middle of everyone's busy work schedule.
- Most unemployed people spend only five hours a week, on average, actively looking for work (according to Lee Hecht Harrison, Inc., a provider of career coaching services). You need to spend six times that to be effective.
- Tell the truth about your situation. Don't be afraid to tell people you were laid off; don't make the mistake I made. Here's what happened: I had become unemployed and found an executive search consultant in Boston who was interested in my experience for a good position. I traveled from Philadelphia to Boston to meet her. At the time of our meeting, I had just been relieved of my responsibilities, and I had a generous salary continuance package. Indeed, technically speaking I was still on the payroll and would remain so for a year. When the question came, "Why do you want to leave your current position as vice president of human resources?" My answer should have been, "Because there is a new president, the fifth one in only seven years, and he wants to pick his own senior leadership team, and I have been advised to look elsewhere." That's what I should have said. I can't remember what I did say, but it doesn't matter because it wasn't true. The interview ended reasonably well, and I left the building. When I was walking back toward the train station, I was overcome with guilt, and I walked back into the building. I had to interrupt the nice lady who had just interviewed me and then I told her the truth. She wasn't happy about what I had done, and I never heard from her again.

There is life—during and after unemployment.
—LAM

If you are employed but trying to make a change, you should be cognizant of nonproductive behaviors.

- It's okay to vent about how much you hate your current job, but don't dwell on it.
- Don't bore your significant other with your complaints about your current job. You'll need his/her input for more important feedback later.
- Use your positive energy for your job search.
- Don't procrastinate; it will drain you, and you'll be stuck in a rut.

Self Help: On the Importance of Quiet Introspection

At the risk of sounding removed from reality, I have found from experience that it's important to sit quietly and just listen. To what? To your intuition, your instincts, your contemplative thoughts and insights—to God's will for you. Now, wait, reader, don't leave me yet. I only ask that you try it. There are many ways to do this. You can develop your own. This is the way I do it.

Every morning I wake up very early. I go to the kitchen and make myself a double espresso. I take my espresso to the living room, sit in a particular chair facing a window in the east, and watch the sunrise (weather and season permitting). During this very quiet time I don't let other noises interrupt. I can see the sun rise for about nine months a year, in this part of upstate New York. In other months, I look out through the window, yes in the dark, at the lights from a hilltop hotel about two miles away. What's all this have to do with "driving high performance strategies and tactics for career decisions"? The point being made is that you should make time for quiet introspection, renewal, reenergizing. This quiet introspection is different than prayer. I often finish my quiet interludes with prayer. In prayer we are often asking for or giving thanks for something. In a quiet interlude, however, the emphasis, the objective is to quiet our minds and spirits—and just listen.

Try it!

You won't need the espresso.

Visualizing the Ideal New Job

Athletes know the value of visualizing. Their coaches train them to visualize details of their performance as if they were actually doing it to enable neurophysiological changes and adaptations, which they will need in actual performance.

As a high-speed motor sport instructor, I use visualization as a technique to practice my own driving techniques—right in my living room! On occasion I sit in a chair, close my eyes, and visualize myself driving my race car at the track. It's important in visualization to include every nuance, every detail. In my case it's getting in my racing seat and adjusting all my safety gear—racing suit, helmet, harnesses, gloves. Turning on the engine, warming up the oil and lubricants, checking all the gauges, easing into first gear, and driving through the paddock to the pits. Then driving out to the pit lane picking up speed in second gear and easing into the track surface in third gear, up the fast right hander climbing the esses at Watkins Glen International Raceway for my warm-up lap. I will do this in my mind for about "three laps," thinking about every turn, every gear change, every braking zone—driving "the perfect lap" in my mind.

The point I'm making here is that the more you can visualize exactly what you want, the greater your chances of increasing the possibilities that this is exactly how things will turn out.

Visualizing, in my experience, has two critical aspects:

a. Visualize exactly what you want, and then
b. *tell people about it!*

If you don't know exactly what you want, then it helps to visualize because in order to accomplish that, you must first do the homework to ascertain what it is that you want in your professional life. By the way, visualization works in many other aspects of life, and it works particularly well for interpersonal relationships. There is a lot more than can be said about visualization techniques, but that's outside the scope of this book.

For purposes of this book and career coaching, the result of your visualization should be a facsimile of an offer letter from the president of the company of your dreams, announcing to everyone that you have been chosen for the job of your dreams with the title and salary of your dreams. For maximum effect the "offer letter" should look as real as possible. It should convey every detail of your career aspirations.

Visualization is not silly. This technique presents a very effective way to help you understand exactly what you want, in the best terms and conditions imaginable to you. This "offer letter" that you're going to type up and hold in your hands should provide you with psychological and emotional support in your career journey, for this document conveys exactly what you want at this point in your career.

But I haven't yet convinced you? You still think it sounds silly? This book that you are now holding in your hands, during its inception, was nothing more than a visualization; actually, it was just my idea of the title page, which later became a concept, then an outline, then a basic manuscript, later a completely edited manuscript, a prototype hardbound book and finally a book for sale nationally through major booksellers.

This tangible book is the direct result of my visualization.

> *These tools are part of the collective unconscious. Lives can be*
> *transformed if people act on these tools.*
> —Jennifer Sertl, Coach to Executives

Here is another example of visualizing in my career. I was once reassigned to a position within a company. I didn't like the new position, the new office, the town where I was being reassigned, not even the nature of the work involved. This caused me to go into a mental funk. But I didn't stay there long because I knew that I was the only one who could get me out of it.

To make way for myself, I visualized my new position in the best possible way. I wrote a two-page document which on the first page described the way I would furnish and decorate the office. This may seem trivial; but given that I would spend ten hours a day, every day in that physical space, I wanted to make sure that it was optimal. I also wanted it to be the best-looking office in the area, which I knew would have the effect of drawing other people with positive energy. On the second page I described the various ways that I would attack the job content, my desired conceptual outcomes of the position, and even the acclaim from others who one day would describe my work product.

The second thing I did was to show that letter to some people that I trusted but were not directly involved in my line of work or even on my work team.

Third, what happened was that within eighteen months it all happened exactly as I described. People today comment that it's the best-looking office in the area, and they like to come in to sit and chat and eat some of the chocolates that I always have on hand.

Everything in that visualization document has come to pass, exactly as described, including the fact that I've already left a legacy of new processes and initiatives in my line of responsibilities that had never been attempted in that company before.

If you are still skeptical, send a message to my Web site, and I'll mail you a copy of that visualization document, which I wrote in April 2006.

On the Importance of Being Balanced

Think of a pyramid. A pyramid has a broad base, and the broader its base, the higher its summit. Now think about a pyramid upside down. It's totally unstable. It can tilt at any moment in any direction, resulting in damage or destruction. The more you know about yourself, the broader is your base, and therefore the higher you can reach. The broader your base, the more you can help others because you are grounded, balanced, rooted. In kung fu (martial arts), balance is all important. If you're not balanced, you cannot effectively defend yourself nor can you attack your opponent. You must first achieve physical balance, be rooted and grounded to be effective.

The same holds true about your persona. Introspection is the tool to accomplish this. Self analysis—not self-criticism—is the route. At one point, I was making a presentation at a conference in Portland, Oregon, when someone in the audience asked, "What if I have trouble with that, with introspection? I don't know how to do that." My response was, "Find a good friend, have a beer with him/her and ask them the question. Tell them that you want some honest feedback about your attributes. A good friend will tell you the truth."

The above advice, about seeking feedback about your attributes, does not include spouses or significant others. Why not ask your spouse? Because they have agendas. They are not bad people, but we all have agendas when we are discussing the attributes of our spouses, significant others or partners. It's important to receive honest feedback but without the added baggage of interpersonal dynamics. If a good friend cannot be found for this purpose, then you may have to pay for professional assessment, using a psychologist, social worker, or other credentialed mental health professional. If they are any good, they will hold up a mirror to your personality.

Growth is the only evidence of life
—John Henry Cardinal Newman

Break Sweat

Do something physical—whatever you like: swimming, biking, power walking, weight lifting, kung fu, pilates, yoga, basketball, etc. The key is *you have to break sweat.* Breaking sweat releases endorphins, which will elevate your mood, your spirits. The more "down" you feel, the more you need to work out.

By the way, sitting at a stationary bicycle and reading a book without a trickle of sweat running down your temple is a complete waste of your time.

There is no substitute for breaking sweat.

And you have dozens of choices on how to do it. Your spouse, significant other, and other loved ones will appreciate it. So will your heart.

Ask for Help

About ten years ago I traveled to San Antonio for a conference. Part of the conference agenda was a golf tournament to benefit a college scholarship fund. In the spirit of participation and camaraderie, I signed up for the tournament even though I rarely play golf (sports car racing is my pastime).

Teams were chosen, and we went out in the wonderful Texas sunshine. As my foursome approached the first tee, I was quite apprehensive about my large handicap. I was very nervous as I addressed the ball. After a couple of awkward practice swings I took a shot, and the ball snaked through the grass for about twenty yards. The members of my group rolled their eyes in dismay. It was going to be a long day.

We bantered and told jokes as we played, but they could scarcely hide their contempt for my lousy game. My score was triple digits by the fifteenth hole. As I addressed the ball for the sixteenth tee, I asked one of the better players, "What am I doing wrong?" He came to where I was standing and helped me with various tips and advice. Heeding his advice, my shots improved significantly for the sixteenth, seventeenth, and eighteenth holes. I felt relieved, and the other guys actually smiled a few times.

I asked my helper, "Why didn't you tell me before?"

He said, "Because you never asked . . ."

What a lesson I learned in that instant.

I still don't play golf, but I have improved in many other areas of importance to me by simply looking for help from those who are successful. With very, very few exceptions, successful people are ready to help. In fact, I have found that the more successful the person is, in any endeavor—in their profession, in their sports or hobbies, or in any other aspect of their life—the more likely they are to extend a hand and help.

If you need help, ask for it.

Your Sunshine Folder

In the course of your job search, you should create a sunshine folder. A sunshine folder is simply a manila folder, preferably bright yellow, where you put thank-you notes, well wishes, e-mails, and other mementos that have been given to you from time to time for things you've done for other people.

What? You don't have any thank-you notes to put in your folder? Well, one of two things is at play: You haven't helped anyone, or you've helped some people, but they haven't had the courtesy to thank you.

You may ask, what's all this have to do with handling rejection? A sunshine folder is a tool that I use when I'm feeling down, for any reason, but it's something that I developed to get me through those long winter months of unemployment.

The sunshine folder reminds you that there are people who do care, and because of that, there is hope.

Performance Management

Not everything that counts can be counted, and not everything that
can be counted counts.
—Albert Einstein

In order to understand what you've done and what remains to be done, you should keep score in some way. Now, as Einstein said, the mistake to avoid is that not everything that can be counted counts. This means that although it's easy to count, for example, how many telephone calls you make in a day, they don't help you if the phone calls you've made are to companies in environments not compatible with your skills, experience, and attributes.

Conversely, the quality of some telephone contacts or even interviews are hard to measure but in fact may carry much more impact and have better predictive qualities, even though those dimensions are difficult to count and characterize.

But measure you must.

Use Excel, if you can, or just a handwritten chart that you can use to track your progress.

- List of networking contacts, with name, address, contact information, notes regarding most recent conversations.
- List of organizations contacted, of positions applied for, of decision makers and recruiters contacted. It's imperative to keep careful notes about what they said so that if there is further contact you can be impressive with your data and project management skills.
- List of interviews, with names and contact information of all persons you met, and notes about each.

By the way, this is not just for your benefit. This is also information that you will use to trade with others in the same circumstances. The better your information gathering and database, the more valuable your "currency," as you go to market to trade with others and help them achieve their job search objectives.

HOMEWORK

1. Visualize yourself in your new position: begin with an introspective sense of self, then your physical environs, and finally the type of work you'll be doing as well as the type of work or tasks you don't want to do.
2. This is your ideal. You may have to make some compromises, but at least you know what you want on several levels and dimensions, not just salary and benefits.
3. Write an announcement memo, as if it were from the president of the desired company to all staff, announcing your new appointment. Include in the visualization memo all aspects of the job. Include the ideal salary (this would not appear on a distributed memo, but it helps you visualize the targeted position).
4. The first part of visualization is to be very specific, so your memo should appear to be the real thing. The second part is to share your vision. Show this memo to everyone you trust.

SEVEN

CAREER DEVELOPMENT
AND DIRECTION

"Open" and "Closed" Vocations

There are some occupations that are "closed," meaning that you cannot perform them because you are not credentialed or licensed. For example, pharmacist, commercial plumber, school psychologist, policewoman, stock broker, dental hygienist, commercial real estate appraiser, etc. You can only pursue those careers if you obtain prescribed training and associated credentials from third parties who officiate over these educational and practice requirements.

The good news is that there are many more occupations that do not require prescribed education, credentialing, or licensing, for example: marketing manager, recruiter, web developer, payroll manager, systems analyst, administrative assistant, event planner, translator, fund raising specialist, etc.

These open occupations, as I call them, afford you countless opportunities for growth and professional development. That's not to say that closed vocations do not lead to growth, but that the growth is at times restricted or constrained by credentialing requirements.

In either case, the path to progress is based on developing and demonstrating a deep (vertical) subject knowledge base. So if you are a network engineer, for example, you would want to immerse yourself in the subject to develop expertise and credibility. Armed with this credibility you can aspire to more responsibility and greater scope of authority—in exchange for promotions and salary increases.

I don't need a concrete sidewalk to get across. I just need some
stepping stones.
—LAM

Why do I state the obvious? Because oftentimes, when a client is stalled in their career and wondering what to do next, they manifest a deep longing to go back to college and get a bachelors or a masters degree in a totally new field.

While desiring to increase one's education may look, on the surface, to have merit, the plan falls short when submitted to scrutiny. They are, in this case, acting more out of desperation, reaching out to whatever solution seems plausible. They sometimes achieve that new educational level only to discover—after significant expense and several years of toil—that they are in the same place as where they started.

Here's a better solution, which I call—climbing the Ts.

Climbing the Ts

Let's use my wife's career path to illustrate this concept. Sharon changed careers several times and is eminently successful in a totally new field—information technology—for which she has had absolutely no formal training. How did she do that?

Applying the concept of climbing the Ts to illustrate her career progress, we can chart when she was climbing the vertical aspect of the T, e.g., learning more and more about a specific subject, and when she moved over to begin another career path, on the horizontal aspect of the T.

When Sharon was in high school, she was training to become a secretary, taking courses in typing and stenography (remember stenography?). Her parents thought she would get a job as a secretary, find somebody to marry, and start her family. That was the conventional wisdom at the time. But Sharon had other plans.

After she graduated from high school, she went back to high school, for a thirteenth grade, to pick up the necessary precollege credits that she had missed. She had been working as a volunteer (candy striper, as they were called) at the local hospital because she really wanted to be a nurse, not a secretary. After finishing thirteenth grade, Sharon then enrolled in the University of Delaware's school of nursing. Four years later, she graduated with a BS in nursing and began work as medical/surgical nurse.

Visualize this: Sharon climbed the first T, the vertical aspect, as she learned more and more about clinical care, especially about cardiology, which was her predilection. She eventually became charge nurse in the cardiac critical care unit, taking care of acutely ill patients. But the rigors of shift rotations were taking their toll, and she decided that she'd rather be a nursing instructor, and thereby have more predictable, more consistent hours of work.

At this point in her career, Sharon was moving on the horizontal aspect of the T, reaching out for an instructor position. Her first teaching position was at a hospital specializing in burns. But Sharon knew nothing about clinical care for burned patients. She had to learn it—quickly! Her first year was very difficult, as she was literally only hours ahead of her students in terms of the subject matter. That is, she would read and learn the clinical care aspects of the burned patient one night and teach the material the next morning. It was very stressful, but she succeeded.

Sharon had been climbing the vertical aspects of burned patient care, learning the specialty. She did that for a couple of years, then she moved to another teaching hospital, but this time for a cardiac care teaching position, which was more of to her liking. Again, she climbed the vertical aspect of the T learning more and more about physiology and cardiology.

When a management position opened for director of critical care, Sharon applied and was promoted. Now, she had to learn to manage hundreds of nurses working the emergency department and in the operating room. While she certainly knew her way around the hospital, managing these many people and large budgets was a totally new experience. Sharon had moved across on the (horizontal) aspect of the T and was now learning the (vertical) subject matter—people management and large complex budgets.

While she was learning this new, complex job, she enrolled in the master's degree program at Villanova University in Pennsylvania. She was now pregnant with our second child, directing the work of hundreds of people, and finishing her master's degree—all at the same time.

When she graduated, she wanted to apply her master's degree to explore the business side of the health care enterprise. Using her experience in directing day-to-day operations of a large hospital, she reached out into a totally different environment and was hired as director of operations for a large for-profit HMO in Philadelphia. So once again, she had gone out on the horizontal aspect of the T to learn something new.

Two things converged which caused her to change career paths. Our third child had been born, and Sharon was overextended with her work responsibilities. In addition, the HMO had run into grave financial difficulties, as in that era there was much turbulence in the healthcare market.

One evening I saw the stress that she was under, and we talked about it. We resolved that it was all right for her to go in the next morning and tell the management that henceforth she would be self-employed, as a consultant to them, so she could control her calendar and her work hours. We were prepared for her to come home without a job. But they wanted her services, so they accepted her terms; and on the spot she became a free agent, a self-employed health care management consultant. We called her new consulting business, The National Resource Group. Sharon had just climbed out unto another horizontal aspect of the T, and now she had to learn how to be successfully self-employed.

The HMO became insolvent, and Sharon shifted her attention as a consultant to a psychiatric hospital facility. Again, reaching out on a horizontal, she had to learn all about psychiatric care, insurance reimbursement, regulatory topics, etc.

We moved to another city as a result of a change in my employment, and Sharon continued to work as a consultant, earning six figures and having to hire an assistant to keep up with the demand for her services. We converted one of the bedrooms into her office as she continued to branch out and learn new services that she could offer. She was climbing the self-employment (vertical) aspect of the T.

After several years we moved to Rochester, New York. There was a dry period of a few years when Sharon was caring for our family, connecting with others and looking for the next passionate opportunity. She was nominated to the board of the e-Business Association while solidifying her vision health care's use of the Internet. In 2004, her work was recognized by the e-Business Association when she was named e-Business Executive of the Year. She eventually landed a position in the marketing department of the University of Rochester Medical Center, responsible for development of the first consumer Web site for the medical center.

When Sharon joined that URMC Marketing team, she had a blue sky idea—that the Web was a very powerful tool, and the medical center should use it to market its clinical services and to create functionality in several aspects of its operations.

Sharon's work with the Web rose quickly to the attention of the URMC leadership. They promoted her to director, Web services, enterprise wide and gave her a significant increase in salary and team and budget to manage.

Sharon went from being an individual contributor to managing a team of seventeen information technology professionals. They are creatively developing software with unique intellectual property and application possibilities for every university hospital in the nation. She has definitely climbed out on the horizontal aspect of the T and is now learning about state-of-the-art IT applications.

Climbing the Ts is about agility. It's about anticipating inexorable change, having a vision, solid attributes, and being prepared for the opportunities as they arise. Climbing the Ts is not only rewarding and refreshing, but it is a required ability in today's complex and ever-changing marketplace. As employers become global in scope, every person must be alert to the trends on the horizon. Everyone must be on the lookout for opportunities to climb the T.

Timing Is (Not Always) Everything!

John Yurkutat and Dorothy Byrne

In 1982, I was interviewed at Hay Associates, a prestigious management consulting firm headquartered in Philadelphia. John and Dotty were managers at the firm, and they offered me a position. I started work there in April, sharing an office with a quirky but very bright fellow. Anyway, as the days turned into weeks, I became concerned and frustrated with the lack of content of my job. I felt that all I was doing was reading and assisting some of the consultants. One of the operations managers resigned from Hay, for another job, and John and Dotty put me in her place. The assignment was called manager, project leaders, and I would supervise seven very bright young graduates of prominent colleges in Philadelphia. It was at this point that John and Dotty informed me that they had originally hired me for what I had to offer (my attributes!) even though at the time they did not have a specific job for me until the operations manager resigned. They hired me at a time when our economy was sour and unemployment was high. Arguably, the timing was poor, in that they did not have a vacancy that I could immediately fill. John and Dotty believed in me to the point of hiring me and placing me on reserve until the right opportunity became evident.

Sometimes You Just Have to Let Go

Don't be my victim
—Jack Welch, Former Chairman, General Electric

Sometimes you have to just walk away. There are times in our career life when getting up in the morning, we can't bear to even think about another day doing an insufferable job. I have been there. And I have quit without a place to go. *This option is not for everybody.* It requires immense internal and supportive resources. But it can be done.

For example, when I worked at Hay Associates in Philadelphia I was busy taking care of client requests for compensation and benefits survey data. But the work culture and the management style at Hay was not agreeable to me. One day I came in and wrote a resignation letter. I wrote, "I hereby resign from Hay Associates effective _____."

I intentionally left the date blank on the resignation letter, hoping that I might be able to negotiate some accommodation. Besides, I had no job to go to.

They asked me why I was quitting. I replied,

> *Look, this is your company, you are the partners and you can certainly run it the way you like. I just can't be a part of it.*
>
> *Where are you going?*
>
> *I don't have another job. Do you want me to clean out my desk?*

I thought they would escort me to the elevator and mail me my personal effects. This is what they had done to others. But they wouldn't let me leave. By tendering my resignation, I had taken the gorilla off my back, and I could feel better about work, so I went back to my office and continued working. On my desk was Project 14, the most important executive compensation project that the company had at that time. This happened during the mainframe era, before PCs were evident on everyone's desk. I had been running all the complicated compensation analyses on the IBM mainframe; and all the data, computations, processes, and formulae were in my head and on my desk. I had built enough of a trust relationship with them that they knew I would never sabotage their business.

About six weeks later, Jack Sosiak called me from Exide Battery Company. He had gone there as the vice president for human resources. He remembered me from working with me at Hay and offered me a position as the manager of compensation and benefits; an offer I gladly accepted.

In the above example, I successfully resigned without another job, from a position where I felt I didn't belong. You may ask why I mention Hay in this experience? Isn't that unkind? Well, no, it's not unkind. I don't have any regrets; I learned a great deal from them, and it's a credit to their management that they let me stay and continue working until I found another job. In the end, it was mutually beneficial, and I have always been proud to have been a part of their team.

Please keep in mind that, as far as I know, at Hay they didn't change any of their practices, certainly not for me. It's important to recognize when to do a strategic withdrawal and not be deluded into thinking that your boss or the company will make changes to mollify you.

But remember—don't be their victim.

On the Importance of Mentors

The most interesting thing on this planet is another human being.
—LAM

Mentors are persons that are interested in helping others. I believe it starts there, with a person who is willing to help. And I believe that the mentee (that's you and me—those who need a mentor) has the burden to look for a mentor. For the relationship to work, the chemistry has to be just right. Both the mentor and mentee need to have the right combination of personality characteristics to make it mutually beneficial. That's why I think it's tough to find a mentor. Mentors are, as we say in Spanish, like *oro molido*, as valuable as gold dust.

Here's a story of a mentor who significantly changed my professional life:

Jack Sosiak

Among the senior consultants dealing directly with the Fortune 500 customers at Hay Associates, there was one—Jack—who was pleasant, confident, and urbane. With a degree from the University of Pennsylvania, his demeanor was impressive. Jack had a rich history of work as a human resource executive with the Campbell Soup Company. I looked up to him and knew him to be wise and savvy. I had not worked with him very much, so my dealings with him were infrequent.

Jack had called me from Exide Battery Company and offered me a position reporting to him as a new manager of compensation and benefits. During my five years at Exide, I traveled widely with Jack. He always had me at his side and was always imparting wisdom and factual knowledge about human resources philosophy and practices and about labor relations, in particular. I have never met a better labor relations executive. His agenda always was to establish trust with the union leaders and always pleasantly but firmly work for the mutual benefit of company and union membership. The balance that he maintained, and the ethical approach he took to labor relations was superb. I can't say enough about Jack in this area.

But it didn't stop there. Although Jack was ten years older than me, he seemed a lifetime more experienced. And best of all, he wanted to share all this with me. We had long conversations, especially when we traveled (and worked sixteen-hour days), where he shared with me his view of the HR world. He not only knew a great deal about human resources and labor relations, but he had also visited many cities in Europe and South America and knew good hotels, good restaurants, good food, good French wine and Cuban cigars. I enjoyed every pearl of wisdom that Jack shared with me.

I consider Jack Sosiak as a great mentor. He helped me tremendously. And he didn't really have to.

EIGHT

ON THE IMPORTANCE OF HELPING OTHERS

I've learned that people will forget what you said, people will forget what you did, but people will never forget how you made them feel.
—Maya Angelou

As I pointed out in previous chapters and as is suggested in many job search publications, networking and joining job clubs are critical to an expedited job search. Invariably, as part of your search process, you will ask favors from others; and you will need contact information about prospects, targeted employers, hiring managers, recruiters, etc. It is therefore paramount that you give, share, and be grateful for the help you receive. Why do I mention the obvious? Well, to be honest with ourselves—because it doesn't always happen.

For example, there was a man that I helped, we'll call him Peter Knudson*, who was unemployed. He heard about me through our church and asked me if we could meet. We met for coffee one morning, and we went through the whole process of CC-101. He told me he was glad we had met and promised that he would do his homework and get back to me.

Weeks went by and I was busy with other clients and with many more activities. One Sunday, I happened to see him at church. I approached him.

Hi Peter. How is it going with you? Did you do any of your career-coaching homework?

Oh, I found a job. I found a good position at a manufacturing company.

He went on to tell me how happy he was. To be honest, I was disappointed. I had spent some of my personal time helping him with his job search at a critical time in his life when he was unemployed and running out of money. But after our initial meeting, he had not made any further contact with me. Peter had accomplished his objective but didn't call or drop me a line to share with me the good news. He had not made himself available for others who are in transition or unemployed.

Please understand that my sentiment about Peter's behavior is disappointment. It's not judgmental. I have no authority to judge his behavior. I'm simply pointing out that it would have been helpful to others if he had shared with me that he had landed a job, had he called me or written me and given me some feedback about how well my process had worked or not worked for him. Mainly, it would have been enormously helpful to get some information about his new employer that we could then use to help others.

I could relate quite a few stories of unrequited assistance. But those would be negative. To accentuate the positive, here is one story about receiving help and paying it forward.

While I was unemployed and in desperate need of cash, I started canvassing for work as a consultant in human resources. I received a tip from George Longshore (of Longshore & Simmons, a consulting company in the Philadelphia area). George was a networking contact that I had made, and he gave me a great tip about a major health care institution in south New Jersey which needed help with compensation strategies and tactics. Armed with some pointers that George gave me, I approached the potential client hospital, and we discussed their business issues and how my skills and experience would meet their needs. They awarded me a contract to overhaul their titles, job descriptions, and compensation structure. We agreed on a professional fee of $15,000, a princely sum to me at that time.

I did the work, and they paid me. It was almost too easy—the part about finding the client work. I had found the client, thanks to George's tip. Naturally, I wanted to show my gratitude to George. So I called him and explained how well things were going with the project. I tried to find a way to compensate him, but he would not accept any remuneration. Other than to refer potential clients to him, I had no real way to pay him back as he would not accept a "finder's fee" from me. I had to find a different way to show my gratitude to George. So here is what I did.

Even before I was finished with that project, another hospital in northern New Jersey had heard about me. I went to see them; we discussed their needs and my experience, and I won that contract as well. Now I had more work than I could handle by myself. I had to find a partner.

Networking through the human resources community of the Tri-State area (Pennsylvania, New Jersey, and Delaware), I found another unemployed HR professional. We'll call him Dave*. He had the compensation expertise that I needed to allow me to work on both client contracts. We made arrangements to meet at a rest stop on the New Jersey Turnpike. After an interview over some coffee, I decided to hire Dave. I hired him as a subcontractor representing my consulting enterprise, the National Resource Group, and we agreed that I could introduce him as my partner to the northern New Jersey hospital. I have to admit that hiring this man was the scariest thing I had ever done because I did not know Dave. However, I needed to make a quick decision and arrangements to satisfy my new client.

Once we agreed to the work arrangements, the compensation arrangements that I made with Dave became my way of "paying forward" my gratitude for what George had done for me. Our conversation about David's compensation at the rest stop on the Turnpike went something like this:

> Dave, I'm confident, based on what I now know about you, that you'll do a good job at the hospital.
>
> Well, thank you, Luis. I'm sure that I can do the work. May I ask now, how will I be compensated?
>
> Here's what I'm thinking, Dave. They have not set a project fee for this contract. Instead, they want to pay as we go, by the hour, until the job is done.
>
> Okay, that's fine. How much are we going to charge them for an hourly rate?
>
> David, that's up to you. You can decide what your worth is to that client, keeping in mind market rates and what the client will bear. When you arrive at a number, say $60 or $100 an hour, or even $1,200 a day, just go ahead and do the work and send them an invoice.

But, Luis, what about you? How do you get compensated as my manager?

Dave, you and I will work on this project together, over the phone and by fax. I'll be behind you the whole time until all the work is completed. To compensate me for my role, all you have to do is—on a biweekly basis—keep 90 percent and send me 10 percent of your gross billings.

Are you sure you only want 10 percent? Wow, that's generous. And how will you know how much I have billed?

Dave, I'm sure you will tell me the truth. I trust you. You'll do the right thing.

Luis, I just never expected that I could keep 90 percent of the billings, that's very generous.

So that's exactly what we did. We worked together on the project for a number of months. Then in July 1996, I began to work my new job at Xerox. I called Dave's home, and his wife, Linda*, answered. I said to her,

Linda, now that I have landed a job at Xerox, there is no need for David to keep sending me any money. He can keep it all. I now have a steady income plus benefits, thank God. David should keep all the gross earnings.

Linda could not believe that I would let David keep everything. She kept thanking me and saying what a wonderful thing this was. All I was doing was paying forward, with gratitude, the tip that George had given me, which allowed me to pay my bills.

> *All human resources practices have already been invented.*
> —LAM

The above story may leave you thinking, *What's so new about giving thanks? Everyone knows one should be grateful and reciprocate.* My sentiments exactly. This and all other aspects of human interaction have been around for millennia. That's not new. What is new is being cognizant of opportunities to help, and then carrying them out.

Here's another way to look at it. I was twelve years old when my parents sent me from Cuba to the United States. They did so out of fear that I would be conscripted into Fidel Castro's militia (People's Army). Arriving by myself in Miami, I stayed with some distant relatives. They enrolled me in seventh grade at Shenandoah Junior High School, and then I waited for my parents to emigrate.

When they arrived in Miami, my father could not find any work as there were hundreds of Cubans arriving every week. The federal government assisted us in moving to a small town—Penn's Grove, New Jersey.

Upon our arrival to that small town, we experienced the loving welcome and endless assistance of the people of Penn's Grove. Here, my father found a job as a janitor in a roadside truck stop, and the folks at Immanuel Methodist Church helped us find an apartment. My sister and I enrolled in school, and we began our new life in the United States.

The way I like to explain it, it's like the people of Penn's Grove put down a ladder for us to be able to climb to where they were. This ladder they put down allowed my father to work, my mother to take care of my sister and me; it allowed us to get an education, to eat a decent meal three times a day, and even to watch a small black-and-white TV.

What I learned from that experience is that I should put ladders down every day, at every opportunity, for others to climb.

> *Luis, I'm just writing to let you know that I found a new job working for the largest bakery supplier in the world. The match was perfect for Holly and me. With this company came a big raise, profit sharing, medical benefits, car (all gas, insurance and maintenance), and a nice 401(k) retirement account. I want to thank you for all your help and the push I needed to get out of my last dead-end job. This new job will grow as I do, allowing me to keep up with our financial demands and enjoy what I do best along the way. Holly and I continue to tell our friends—you have helped many lives and families more than you will ever know! Thanks again.*

—Michael Malley, Sales Professional

Love all.
Trust a few.
Hurt none.

—William Shakespeare

ATTACHMENT A

LOVE TO DO

Skills   *Attributes*

ATTACHMENT B

EXAMPLES OF ELEVATOR SPEECHES

- *Results oriented leader with proven success analyzing markets and businesses, identifying market opportunities, and developing strategies to leverage competitive advantage. Adept in developing innovative solutions to multidimensional problems. Uncommon ability to learn quickly to rapidly distill complex business problems to their core issues. Very curious and critical thinker who can apply extensive experience from a variety of industries to drive revenue growth and profitability. Effective speaker to C-level audiences, directors, and large groups.*

(This management consultant for the renewable resources industry said that he had sent out "zillions" of cover letters and resumes, with no results. He has a PhD in engineering plus an MBA. We met for CC-101, discussed how to present his attributes in his cover letter and resume. He sent one new cover letter and resume, emphasizing his attributes—not just his skills and experience—and the targeted company called him three times the following day. He and his wife were incredulous.)

- *Enterprising and articulate business professional with the proven ability to manage multiple tasks and accomplish objectives in a fast-paced environment. Customer-oriented individual with outstanding communication, organizational, and interpersonal skills demonstrated by the ability to work with people of diverse backgrounds. Experience with providing written and oral business presentations.*

(This is the elevator speech of Donna Highsmith, thirty-two years old, who landed a well-paid position as internal communications director for a national security company in Florida's Gold Coast.)

- *Results-driven, enthusiastic, tenacious office management professional desiring opportunity to utilize my skills, experience, and attributes to generate revenue and maintain customer relationships, contract administration, and process optimization for professional services organization.*

(With only a high school education, Tara accepted a supervisor's position at a blue chip company paying $55,000.)

- *Articulate, well-organized consulting professional with business-to-business experience and particular skills in relationship building, business and project analysis, and customer management. Excellent track record with sales performance, consultation, and achieving market penetration.*

- *Mature, punctual college student seeking summer full-time and school year part-time employment to defray college expenses. Detail oriented, mechanically inclined with strong customer service skills. Demonstrates exceptional problem-solving abilities, enjoys working in teams, and is very logical.*

(This twenty-year-old high school graduate landed an entry level technical position with a nationally renowned Porsche racing engine rebuilding business.)

- *Creative, dedicated, and passionate music educator, offering effective communications with exceptional musicianship, teaching, and presentation skills; high degree of professionalism, decision making, and problem solving; superior project design and program management; supervisory experience; appreciation for aesthetics, eye and ear for detail; versatility and human compassion.*

(This music educator was not receiving any responses to her resumes until she included language about her attributes in her elevator speech and in her cover letter.)

- *Resourceful, enthusiastic, and entrepreneurial human resources leader with demonstrable accomplishments as strategic partner to senior leaders of manufacturing, healthcare, academic, business services, multiunion and multinational enterprises. Seeking opportunity in organization needing seasoned trusted advisor and operational leader for growth.*

(Successful human resources consultant.)

- *Effective leader in development strategies that support business growth. Accomplished training and development program manager and facilitator with experience in development, deployment and administration of training solutions that get results. Recognized as exceptional organizer with strong project and people management skills. Engaging interpersonal style, process oriented, and effective at building coalitions. Consistent record as a customer satisfaction enabler with business maturity and a solid work ethic.*

(Very successful international training professional wielding "big company" ideas with small group delivery.)

- *Dynamic, results-oriented leader with proven success in analyzing customer and business needs and developing strategies that support high-growth environments. Customer oriented, without outstanding communications and interpersonal skills. Recognized ability to work across boundaries and motivate teams to drive innovative solutions to multidimensional problems. Resourceful, critical thinker who can apply extensive experience from a variety of disciplines to derive operational excellence worldwide.*

(Seasoned Fortune 500 quality, service and support manager)

ATTACHMENT C

COVER LETTER TEMPLATE

Your Name
Your Address
City, State Zip
Telephone   **Email address**

Prospect Name
Prospect Title
Address
City, State, Zip

Today's Date

Dear _____,

    I was referred to you by _____. My purpose in writing is to explore how my skills [name some], experience [name some], and personal attributes [name two] may be of value to _____ [company name].

    Your organization is of great interest to me because I have been [briefly explain relevant skills and experience to the target opportunity]. As you can see in my resume (enclosed) in my work I love to [briefly describe those things that you love to do in your current or past employment]. My customers [or clients or peers or managers] say that I have a passion for _____, and that they can see that I love to _____.

    Perhaps your organization can take advantage of my [attribute], [attribute], and [attribute] to [improve sales/improve customer satisfaction/reduce cost/improve margins]. I will be calling your office on [date and time] to follow up.

Sincerely,
Your Name
/enc.

ATTACHMENT D

JUNE FARNSWORTH
1520 Ethereal Crescent
Farnorth, New York 17869

Home 598/987-6842
Cell 598/869/7480
myhouse@yahoo.rr.com

CAREER SUMMARY

Effective **leader in development strategies that support business growth**. Accomplished training and development program manager and facilitator with experience in the development, deployment, and administration of training solutions that get results. Recognized as an exceptional organizer with strong project and people management skills. Engaging interpersonal style, process oriented, and effective at building coalitions. Consistent record as a customer satisfaction enabler with business maturity and a solid work ethic.

PROFESSIONAL EXPERIENCE
FAROUT CORPORATION, Farnorth, New York 1984-2006

Development Manager, Developing Operations 2004-2006

Managed the development function for an organization of 9000 direct and indirect employees across 104 countries in Latin America and Eastern Europe. Built a direct team of US-based development program managers and a global network of regional training and development managers. Improved the capability of overseas sales populations through the deployment of effective and efficient development principles, practices, and tools. Created development standards, expectations, and measurements that built employee competencies and an environment of continuous learning. Provided courses and learning materials that enabled effective field deployment to bridge the skills and performance gaps toward advancing our business objectives.

- Created standardized job profiles and learning paths for field sales, sales management, and technical roles.
- Established a global development network for consistent deployment of training programs, across geographies with varying levels of training support, delivery capability, and learning practices.
- Implemented a sales management process and training program, which improved consistency of sales tracking and support processes.
- Created an annual training plan delivery metrics and process, which enabled the support and inspection of training delivery required to build needed skills and competencies.
- Facilitated steps toward a global management and leadership development by coordinating sharing among various FAROUT development groups that create similar programs for their specific geographies.
- Respected participant on the human resources leadership team.

Manager, Launch, Learning, and Communications for field technical sales population 2000-2003

Managed team of six launch managers who rolled out new products and solutions to field populations. Developed and communicated product support strategies to technical sales support populations.

- Designed and implemented processes to ensure technical sales force had reliable methods to obtain the technical and marketing information they needed to support the sales cycle. Provided field-training strategy/direction.
- Expedited field sales support training by collecting requirements and engaging the education organization to create alternative solutions that could be delivered earlier than standard programs, addressing significant knowledge gaps caused by staff reductions.

Manager, Technical Operations Programs and Strategies 1998-2000

Managed a team of five direct reports who created and implemented product launch programs for a newly formed technical field organization.

- Redesigned field customer trainer job structure to reflect increase in technical skill levels required to support networked products. Assessed and reassigned each trainer against these new job requirements to ensure that their title and grade accurately reflected their current experience and skill level.

Manager, Customer Education Marketing and Development Programs 1996-1998

Managed six direct reports who created marketing collaterals, customer training materials and implemented marketing programs for field and training organizations.

- Reduced training materials development costs by 10 percent.
- Reversed wave of customer dissatisfaction by standardizing product training outputs and materials across all product development teams and in ten different countries.

Manager, Customer Education National Reprographic Program 1994-1995

Managed four direct reports who designed and rolled out new fee-based training program for reprographic products.

- Defined field training job responsibilities, grade levels, compensation structure, and training plans.
- Created and tracked revenue plans for this new line of business and created manpower and contracting plans.
- Enhanced the ability to attract higher skilled trainers by convincing senior management of the need to convert nonexempt field trainer jobs to exempt levels. This was critical to justify the new practice of charging customers for training that had previously been provided free of charge.

Manager, Customer Education Marketing 1993

Managed ten direct reports who developed marketing collaterals that were used by external and internal customers to understand the choices and benefits of training offerings. Represented the San Francisco based customer education organization in Farnorth headquarters and acted as liaison for all functions.

Manager, Customer Education Training Development, Los Angeles, California 1988-1992

Managed a team of fifteen training developers who created customer training instructor guides and student workbooks used to deliver fee-based customer training on systems products. Supplied all Farout operating divisions with documentation and training materials for output, internal, and outsourced product manufacturing.

Training Analyst, San Diego, California 1983-1987

Wrote printing systems operator guides and training materials used by field analysts to train customers. Delivered train-the-trainer sessions to new-hire analyst classes.

PRIOR EXPERIENCE

LAIDBACK CENTER and LIFESTYLES, INC., Sausalito, California 1977-1982

Hired, trained, and managed sales and delivery staff of fifteen for a retail furniture store. Sold furniture and provided decorating services to customers who purchased substantial orders.

ADVANCED DEVELOPMENT CENTER, Laguna Beach, California 1974-1976

Developed individualized lesson plans and taught students who were experiencing self-concept challenges in Southern Beach School District kindergarten or private preschool programs.

EDUCATION AND COMPUTER SKILLS
BA Psychology, Domain University, California, 1977
Microsoft Office Suite: Word, PowerPoint, Excel

PROFESSIONAL ASSOCIATION
National and local Member of America Society of Training and
Development (ASTD)
Vice President of Professional Development Programs for Farnorth ASTD

ATTACHMENT E

THE TEE CHART FOR INTERVIEWING

What do they want/need?	What can I offer/contribute?

ATTACHMENT F

COLD NETWORKING CALL

- Hello, my name is _____.
- _____ suggested I give you a call. S/he felt that you would be a good person to offer me some tips or advice.
- I know you are very busy, so I won't take up too much of your time.
- I am in a career transition at this time, and I am interested in how businesses that you know handle their *[problems with which you have skills and expertise]*.
- May I set up a short meeting with you, at your convenience, to obtain your feedback about the types of industries and companies that I am targeting in my search?
- _____ thought you could be very helpful to me in this way.
- You can call me at my number, _____. I will also send you an e-mail with my contact information, in case that works better for you.
- Thank you, and I look forward to meeting with you.

ATTACHMENT G

Warm Networking Call

- Hello, this is _____. You may recall, we know each other from _____.
- I know you are very busy, so I won't take up too much of your time, but I was thinking that you would be a good person to offer me some suggestions.
- Currently I am in career transition, and I am interested in how other organizations in the _____ area manage their *[problems about which you, the reader, have skills and experience].*
- With your permission I would like to set up a short meeting with you, at your convenience, to obtain your perspectives and insights about the industries that I am targeting.
- If you'd like, you can call me at my number, _____. I will also send you an e-mail with my contact information, in case that works better for you.
- Thank you, and I look forward to meeting with you!

APPENDIX

Attributes	
Academic	Intelligent
Active	Introspective
Action oriented	It's a jungle out there
Accurate, detailed	Investigative/measured
Adaptable	Leader
Adventurous	Low profile
Aggressive	Loyal
Ambitious	Mellow, quiet
Analytical	Motivated
Artistic	Needs prodding, deadlines
Assertive	Open minded
Balanced	Optimistic
Broad picture	Orderly
Calm	Organized
Capable	Passionate
Caring	Passive
Cautious	Patient
Communicative	Perceptive
Compassionate	Personable

Competitive	Persevering
Confident	Politically savvy
Conscientious	Positive
Conservative	Precise
Contemplative	Prefer structure, process
Creative	Problem solver
Dependent on structure	Progressive
Determined	Prudent
Energetic	Quick study
Enthusiastic	Reliable
Entrepreneurial	Responsive/Quick
Ethical	Results oriented
Expressive	Risk adverse
Flexible	Risk taker
Focused	Satisfied
Follower	Self controlled / managed
Fun	Self starter
Goal oriented	Serious
High Tolerance for Ambiguity	Shy
Highly energized	Sociable
Initiates	Solo practitioner
Honesty	Spontaneous
Humorous	Strategic
Imaginative	Visionary
Innovative	Withdrawn / introverted
Inscrutable	Witty

SUGGESTED READING

Mitch Albom, *Tuesdays with Morrie: An Old Man, a Young Man, and Life's Greatest Lesson* (Broadway Books, 1997)

Richard Bolles, *What Color is Your Parachute? A Practical Guide for Job-Hunters and Career Changers.* (Berkeley: Ten Speed Press, 2006).

Timothy Butler, *Getting Unstuck: How Dead Ends Become New Paths* (Boston: Harvard Business School Press, 2007)

Napoleon Hill, *Think and Grow Rich* (Ballantine Books, 1960)

W. Chan Kim and Reneé Mauborgne, *Blue Ocean Strategy: How to Create Uncontested Market Space and Make the Competition Irrelevant* (Harvard Business School Press, 2005)

Dan Miller, *48 Days to the Work You Love* (Tennessee: B&H Publishing Group, 2007)

Orville Pierson, *The Unwritten Rules of the Highly Effective Job Search: The Proven Program Used by the World's Leading Career Services Company* (New York: McGraw Hill, 2006)

Susan Scott, *Fierce Conversations: Achieving Success at Work & in Life, One Conversation at a Time* (New York: Viking, 2002)

Paul Tieger and Barbara Barron. *Do What You Are : Discover the Perfect Career for You Through the Secrets of Personality Type* (3rd ed. 2001)

Michael Watkins, *The First 90 Days: Critical Success Strategies for New Leaders at All Levels* (Boston: Harvard Business School Publishing, 2003)

NOTES AND REFERENCES

(NB: It is with utmost sadness that I report that while I was drafting this book, I discovered that George Longshore was killed in Washington DC. George was taken from us way too soon. My sincerest condolences to his wife and family.)

Alan Breznick, *Mastering the Art of Selection* (Cornell Enterprise, fall 2004)

Perri Capell, *The Right Time to Talk About Salary* (The Wall Street Journal OnLine, January 23, 2007)

Cornell Career Services. *Career Guide 2005/2006* (Ithaca, NY: Cornell Career Services, Cornell University)

Carlos Eire, *Waiting for Snow in Havana: Confessions of a Cuban Boy* (The Free Press, 2003)

Cheryl Gilman, *Doing Work You Love: Discovering Your Purpose and Realizing Your Dreams* (Barnes & Noble/McGraw Hill, 1997)

Fali Huang, and Peter Cappelli. *Employee Screening: Theory and Evidence. http://papers.nber.org/papers/w12071.pdf* (accessed March 2006).

Steve Jobs, *Commencement Address* (Stanford, CA: Stanford University, June 16, 2005)

Spencer Johnson, *Who Moved My Cheese? An Amazing Way to Deal with Change in Your Work and in Your Life* (New York: G. P. Putnam's Sons, 1998)

Orville Pierson, *The Unwritten Rules of Highly Effective Job Search.* (McGraw Hill, 2006)

Rosa Smith-Montanaro, *Mind Over Platter—Train Your Brain To Think Thin!* (Rochester, NY: 2006)

Kevin Wheeler, *A Letter to Hiring Managers: How to Make Sure You Hire the Best—Five Tips for You as You Work with Your Recruiters* (ERE Daily, September 8, 2006)

"What are the top three rules for jobseekers to follow to successfully negotiate the best possible compensation package?" *http://womenforhire.com.*

Michael D. Zinn, *Executive Search Newsletter,* Volume XVII, Edition I, (Lawrenceville, NJ February 2006)

INDEX

D

deal busters, 24
Dell, 77
Dell, Michael, 77
diminishing returns, 14, 15
Dunn & Bradstreet, 61

E

Edison, Thomas A., 109
Einstein, Albert, 116
Eire, Carlos
    Waiting for Snow in Havana:
        Confessions of a Cuban Boy, 9
electronic mail. *See* e-mail
elevator speech, 14, 49, 51, 52, 65,
    69, 90
    examples of, 135, 136, 137
e-mail, 90, 100
emotional hook, 56
environments, 21
Evans, Rachelle, 92
Execunet, 62
Exide Battery Company, 125, 126
exploratory interview, 81

F

FedEx, 77

G

Garman, Tom, 40
Gates, Bill, 77
Golisano, Tom, 77
Google, 60, 61

H

Hay Associates, 49, 123, 124
headhunters, 88, 89
heart, 26
high school graduates, 24
hobbies, 26
Huang, Fali, 34
Huston, Samuel R., 43

I

illegal questions, 72, 73
industries, 28, 63
Ingen, Michael Van, 48
instinct, 32, 111
intelligence, 33
interests, 18, 26
Internet, 77, 89, 94
interview, 67
    exploratory, 86
    telephone, 83, 84
    tools, 68, 69
interview questions, 70, 71, 72
interviewing
    do's and don't's, 77, 78, 79
introspection, 111, 114

J

job lead, 61
job search, 13
Jobs, Steve, 18, 37, 77
Johnson, Denise, 21
Johnson, Spencer, 103

K

knowledge, skills, and attributes, 42
KSAs. *See* knowledge, skills, and
    attributes
Kung fu, 114,115

L

layoffs, 109
Lee Hecht Harrison, Inc., 110
LinkedIn, 63
Longshore, George, 128
love, 26, 57
love to do, 27

M

Magin, Cheri, 99
Malley, Michael, 131
Martínez, Sharon, 120-123
Maynard, Ann, 84
MBTI (Myers-Briggs Type
    Indicator), 22
McKay, Harvey, 28
mentors, 125
Microsoft, 77
momentum, 59

N

National Bureau of Economic
    Research, 34
Navajas, Peggy Ann, 61
negotiating, 95
networking, 62, 63, 88
Newman, John Henry Cardinal, 114

O

objective, 51, 52
obstacles, 40
open vocations, 119

P

PAETEC, 69
passion, 26, 57
Paychex, 77
paying forward, 129
Peale, Norman Vincent, 17
performance management, 116
perquisites, 14
Pierson, Orville, 80
Poisson, Nancy, 46
positions, 20, 27
predictors, 34
professional self, 29
promotion, 119

R

recruiters, 32, 37, 63
    contingency, 88
    corporate, 37
rejection, 80
results, 101
resume, 14, 31, 35, 52
    chronological, 53
    competent, 52, 53
retained search, 89
Rickley, Porter S., 42, 43
Rock, Milton L., 49